INTRODUCTION

GAME ON

"In the beginning we only flirted with martial art movies, but it wasn't until Bruce lee came along that we fell in love with them"
Rick Baker

In this standalone hardback collector's edition, I have collaborated with film maker Alan Canvan. Back in 2018 I did an exclusive preview in London of his re edited cut of "The Game of Death Redux". Jump forward to 2022 and Alan has taken his cut to the next level of the pagoda.

In this issue I and Alan discuss in depth "Redux 2.0" and we hope though our dialogue we can bring observations that some readers may not have picked up on during their viewing of the movie. When a new cut of any film is presented most people are searching for new footage, for Example whenever I discuss "The Game of Death" amongst Bruce Lee fans their opening words are "has it got the Dan Inasanto log sequence" or "any of the outside footage Bruce that was filmed". The answer is NO! Personally I would love to have seen these sequences restored and added to any final cut, but these missing scenes do not in any way detract from what Alan has accomplished.

THE LOG SCENE

A scene in which Chieh Yuan's character and Dan Inosanto's character fight each other before James Tien's character and Bruce Lee's character arrive. This is known is more commonly known as "The Log Scene" because Chieh Yuan's character is wielding a log during the fight. This scene is reportedly lost with the only known prints of the scene being in Director Stephen Tong and Dan Inosanto's possession. Despite the many rumours of this footage being located like the "saw in the head" missing scene in the "Big Boss" 50 years on nothing has ever materialised to give credit to the rumours.

I truly believe the footage exists! but money does not seem to temp those that have it their possession to come forward and allow it to be shown to the world. Before I started talking to Alan I had my theories on Bruce's uncompleted movie, but I have to admit spending hours on zoom with Alan has totally re-educated me and I find myself now listing "The Game

of Death" as my favourite Bruce Lee movie over "Enter the Dragon"

It is my hope that like me, people will view Alan's "Game of Death Redux 2.0" with a fresh pair of eyes. And conversations that spring up on social media will allow people to have a greater understanding of this piece of cinematic art and Alan's achievements bringing his vision to be the most complete version that you are ever likely to see. The book will be out before people get a chance to watch this new updated edit. Giving the reader a chance to familiarise themselves with what Alan has achieved with his dedication and passion that took over three years to get it to a point that he was satisfied. Creating, a personal vision, with the materials he had available.

I would like personally thank Alan for helping make this issue possible with his cooperation and time and for enlightening me on the finer points of "The Game of Death"

PLAYING THE GAME

Interview with ALAN CANVAN

By Rick Baker

"There is never an excuse not to finish a film." - Werner Herzog

RB: Before we start Alan can I ask you a little about your background as a filmmaker and what got you into Bruce Lee and the first movie you saw and the impact it had on you?

AC: I'm a child of the 70s and 80s, who was raised on a steady diet of movies, television and comic books. When I was seven years old, I saw my first image of Bruce Lee in a magazine while listening to my cousin give me a scene-by-scene synopsis of The Big Boss. I spent the following two years tracking Lee through newspaper clippings and fanzines until I was finally able to see him on the big screen in the Summer of 1979. Fittingly, my cinematic introduction was Game of Death. I walked out of the movie theater feeling like somehow the world had changed. The effect he had on my childhood can't be overstated. Despite the movie's patchiness, it was part of a ternary of films that made me fall in love with cinema as an art form. For the last three decades I've been involved in the film world to varying degrees as an actor, writer, and director, although I consider that peripheral to being just a huge lover of movies.

RB: It's great to catch up with you again Alan. I'll start by going back to 2019 when you were kind enough to allow me to screen the working print of Game of Death Redux to an audience at my Kung Fu Cafe in Stratford, London. It was very well received by the audience, and I wanted to ask what happened next on your journey?

AC: That was a cool opportunity for me to share my then work in progress with the UK fans. Kudos, Ricky, for hosting the event immediately after I debuted it at the Asian American Asian Research Institute in New York. Following the initial screenings, I jumped right back in the firepit and continued to refine my edit for another six months. In the interim, producer Curtis Tsui at Criterion learned of my project and expressed interest in seeing my work. He fell in love with Redux and we struck a deal to include it on their 2020 box set. Having the premiere home video distribution company deem my work worthy of their platform was a true Cinderella moment.

RB: So, your version was picked up by Criterion and I believe the version that appears on it is a slightly shorter version than the working print I had screened. Can you tell me what cuts you made for the box set release?

AC: The main changes involved switching out SD shots for HD shots wherever I could, though I did snip several excess frames in certain sequences to tighten up the overall flow the film. The current version is a full restoration that upscales the remaining SD footage, gives it a new color grade and reworks the entire audio design. I also restructured some music cues and a few cross-cuts. "Chiseling away at the unessential" was my guiding principle as each iteration of the edit brought me closer to the dramatic narrative that I knew existed within the material. I'm a firm believer that certain stories have a life of their own and, at times, the narrative in Game of Death knew better than me how it needed to manifest. The sculpture slowly revealed itself over the two-years it took me to complete the project. Redux currently has the shortest running time of all the edits including the work print version that you screened almost three years ago. Not including the written prologue and end credits the footage currently clocks in at thirty minutes and ten seconds.

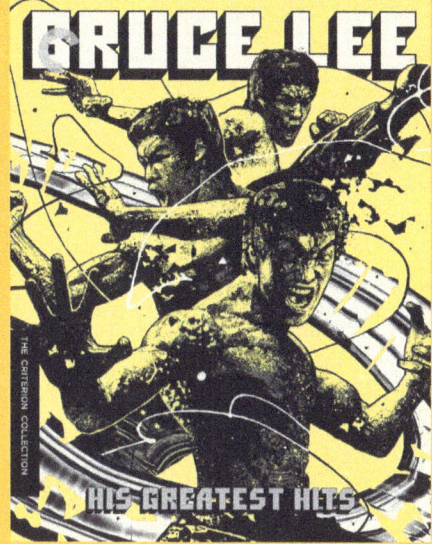

RB: Music placed in the wrong sequences can change the mood completely as to what the director is trying to achieve. How important were the music cues to create the right atmosphere?

AC: The music score was paramount. In film, the resonance of a scene is often driven by a combination of sound and image working in unison to unconsciously elicit a particular emotion in the viewer. Great composers, at heart, are great storytellers who relay stories through their compositions. John Barry's score for Game of Death is note-perfect in its ability to sonically communicate the intricacies of the physical battles within the pagoda while simultaneously delivering a magnific theme that encompasses the larger narrative. With Redux, it was important to me that each floor had a distinct sonic identity that reflected a thematic colour: Yellow, for the Hall of the Tiger; Red, for the Hall of the Dragon; Black, for the Hall of the Unknown. Equally as important was allowing the soundtrack to address the link between specific characters. An example of this is the percussion that accompanies Hai Tien's arrival on the second floor which I later use to introduce Jabbar.

RB: I feel that in this interview, we must pay much respect to John Barry. His score without doubt compliments the flow, and the tension with the perfect rhythm of Bruce Lee on screen art. If I searched for a soundtrack for the rest of my life, it would fail to come close to this masterpiece.

AC: From the beginning, I've stressed that Redux is as much a tribute to John Barry's artistry as it is to Bruce Lee's genius. His music plays a pivotal role in the presentation of the footage and gives Lee's work a magnitude that's truly worthy of its brilliance. An expanded edition of the soundtrack is long overdue, as there are several pieces of music in the 1978 film that I would have loved to include in Redux, that didn't make it on to the official release.

RB: What inspired you to go back and rework your original cut and create Game of Death Redux 2.0?

AC: Really, it was the opportunity to restore the footage in a way that reflected my aesthetic as a filmmaker. I'd like Game of Death to be recognized for the artistic piece it is, rather than an afterthought that's relegated to the 'what could have been' file. Also, as a fan, I wanted the best possible presentation of the film on Blu-Ray.

RB: For a long time, Game of Death was dismissed by Bruce fans as just an unfinished movie. But in more recent times people are now viewing it with a different pair of eyes, often making it there favourite movie after Enter the Dragon, especially for the Japanese audience. Do you think since the additional footage was found by Bey Logan at the vaults of Star Video (Media Asia) and re-edited by various people including your original version that this is a reason for its sudden appeal amongst fans?

AC: I think its appeal is multi-factorial. Game of Death possesses a visual aesthetic unlike any motion picture that's come before or after it. There's an unconventional expression to the set design and costumes that would fit comfortably in a David Lynch film. That the movie was never finished gives the footage an amorphous quality which demands that the audience engage their imagination. I believe that's integral to why it continues to fascinate.

RB: Since the internet has become the main source now to debate Bruce Lee in forums and more information keeps appearing pertaining to Game of Death. Did you get into any of the debates or look at the many theories that have appeared and take from their suggestions?

AC: I do my best to refrain from engaging in online debates. Most forums are just breeding grounds for armchair quarterbacks — most of whom wouldn't know good storytelling if it hit them smack in the face with a two-by-four. The wonderful thing about bluntness is it gauges the strong and intimidates the weak.

RB: So, would it be fair to assume that Redux is a pure work on your understandings as a filmmaker?

AC: Redux started out as an extended remix of the eleven-minute edit Robert Clouse put together for his 1978 movie. Somewhere along the way it became something else — something reflective of my sensibilities as a filmmaker. Though it borrows certain elements from the Game of Death 1978 film, Redux is a direct expression of my interpretation of Lee's work. One thing I emphasize in that interpretation is the notion that the footage works perfectly as a self-contained short film without requiring additional elements to make it feel complete. That alone, differentiates it from the previous offerings.

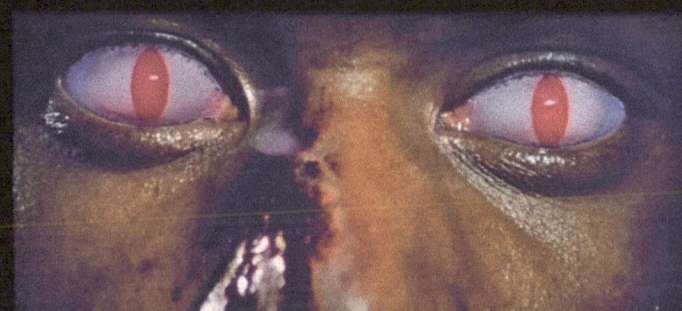

RB: Up until now, apart from your new edit, what, for you, was the purest cut of Game of Death footage you had seen and why?

AC: Of the three versions that precede mine, Alan Pattillo's eleven-minute edit of the Game of Death '78 sequence comes the closest to Lee's sensibilities as a storyteller. Barring Redux, its, by far, the most dramatic presentation of the material. Audiences often don't consider that a film is made three times: first, when the screenwriter commits the story to paper; second, when the director, actors and crew shoot the film; and finally, when the editor constructs the story in real time. The final stage is, in many ways, the most crucial, though least discussed, aspect of filmmaking. With the 1978 film, Pattillo pieced together a sequence that truly showcased the importance of the editing process to how Bruce Lee's battles came across on screen. There's also something to be said for the fact that the production was steered by professional filmmakers who understood how pacing and soundtrack affect a narrative.

RB: Let's go back to the first time you saw the full Game of Death footage in 2000 and your thoughts then as to what Bruce was trying to get across to the audience verses now?

AC: Like many fans, my initial take away was Lee's sermon on the nature of adaptability. The reframe came later when I began reflecting on Kareem's role and how the reveal of his character's eyes anchored the central theme of the story. At the time, fan's speculated that Jabbar's character was meant to be a vampire, mutant, science experiment etc. Some believed that Bruce was shooting the first martial arts sci-fi flick. None of those explanations resonated with me, and as I delved deeper into Bruce's ideas — particularly the ones for the Silent

RB: Kareem Abdul-Jabbar Has been interviewed on many occasions but never, to my knowledge, has he been asked about who his character was meant to be or whether he was to have the lizard eyes or just regular eyes. I would love to hear your thoughts on this and what you feel Bruce was trying to achieve for the audience?

AC: Well, Jabbar's character is really a physical manifestation of Hai Tien's dark side. This archetype, known as the 'shadow self', was identified by Swiss psychiatrist Carl Jung, whose writings influenced Lee and Stirling Silliphant's ideas for The Silent Flute. Bruce recognized the inherent symbolism in Jung's work and found that the Jungian landscape lent itself to dynamic storytelling. He chose to shape the pagoda sequence around these concepts. This involved designing a specific visual motif for Kareem's character which included opaque sunglasses, long limbs and a dark room illuminated by candlelight. These hallmarks informed my choice to use the lizard eyes rather than the normal ones. It's appropriate that Hai Tien and Jabbar's battle is framed in darkness, as the struggle is an allegorical portrait of man confronting his deepest fear. I'll also point out that there's significance in the fact that Kareem's character consumes James Tien's character, who is essentially paralyzed by his fear, whereas Hai Tien embraces his doubts and is transformed as a result.

RB: If I remember correctly, in John Little's book he referred to Kareem as "Mantis". What are your thoughts on this, and do you agree?

AC: John did a considerable amount of guess work to arrive at that conclusion. It doesn't appear that he had any real understanding of Kareem's character. The thought dialogue segments in Lee's notes were written in Cantonese – a language with many intricacies that do not necessarily translate well to English, so his attempt at deciphering the words were speculatory at best. Kareem was the guardian of the Hall of the Unknown so, contextually, it makes no sense for him to have a name. If he were to have one, Hakim, which means "the Judge" in Arabic, would, ironically, be much more fitting. Although the Jungian subtext wasn't directly addressed in Lee's notes, its footprints (pun intended!) are all over the material. Let me know if you need examples.

RB: Yeah, please highlight a few examples.

AC: There's a moment when Hai Tien arrives on Kareem's floor, stops dead in his tracks and slowly raises his head up in awe of the bigger man's size. The corresponding shot sees Jabbar lift his head derisively in almost the same manner. The movements between them in that instance suggest a reflection, comparable to a distorted image you would see in funhouse mirror.

RB: Yes. I remember that.

AC: Why did Lee have Jabbar respond like that? Later in the battle, there's the marvelously operatic sequence where Hai Tien discovers Kareem's weakness and pops out the window screens to literally and figuratively bring light into the darkness. Subtle, it's not (laughter). Of course, the concept of confronting one's shadow self was not unique to Lee, having been explored in numerous works of literature and art such as Frankenstein, Dr. Jekyll and Mr. Hyde, The Incredible Hulk, Star Wars and many more. It's the stuff of great art.

RB: What are your thoughts on the framed scene where we see Jabbar's character cast a spindly shadow against wall? Intentional or incidental?

AC: Yes, I call it the Nosferatu shot, as it draws heavily from F.W. Murnau's 1922 classic film of the same name. The movie is known for being one of the earliest examples of German Expressionism in cinema and uses techniques such as crisp shadows, exaggerated angles and distinct physical traits to convey the emotional state of a character or situation, as opposed to replicating straight realism. The long shot of Kareem pulling off his robe and projecting a massive shadow onto the wall is a perfect illustration of Lee's use of Expressionism throughout the film and optically plays on the idea

of the shadow self. One thing that I try to convey in Redux is the suggestion that the battle with Jabbar, as well as the other guardians, is dualistic. While the fights do take place in the 'real world' of the narrative, they also represent Hai Tien's inner battle with aspects of his own subconscious and, through confronting them, he comes to better understand who he is as a warrior and as an individual. According to Jung, the encounter brings with it "the danger of falling victim to the shadow ... the black shadow which everybody carries with him, the inferior and therefore hidden aspect of the personality." In Kareem's case, the dark room and eyes metaphorically personify everything Hai Tien, thus far, has refused to acknowledge about himself.

RB: Back in the 70's when Bruce Lee was starting to sweep across the UK, I remember buying various magazines featuring Lee including Kung Fu Monthly. When we first started seeing pictures of the yet unreleased Game of Death, I was totally amazed at seeing Bruce in a yellow cat suit. This was to instantly become iconic amongst his fans, and replica suits were soon in every martial arts shop. In Game of Death, we see early in the fight scene, Jabbar kicking Bruce in the chest with his foot, and, as Bruce gathers his composure, we see the foot imprint on Bruce Lee's catsuit. I would love to get your thoughts on this a filmmaker.

AC: The black footprint on Lee's yellow tracksuit is one of those moments in cinema that takes full advantage of the inherent theatricality in German Expressionism. While the footprint is real in the sense of the physical realm, it's equally symbolic of the indelible trace of the shadow on the human subconscious. From that perspective, the imprint of Jabbar's foot on the tracksuit figuratively becomes a Rorschach test. Coming at it from another angle, the design is truly indicative of Lee's wicked sense of humor! Here, his commitment to the abstract tows the line of pop art. Andy Warhol had nothing (laughter).

RB: What are your thoughts on Warrior's Journey being indicative of Bruce's vision because John Little was going by Bruce's specified shot list and notes versus the 1978 and Art Port versions?

AC: A good number of the takes in Warriors Journey were inferior to those used in both the 1978 film and Art Port edit. It's doubtful that Lee would have picked those shots. But even if I accepted that they were in accordance with Lee's notes, there remains a fundamental issue to consider which is, the notes, at the end of the day, are nothing more than that — just notes. Fans tend to view them as gospel when, from a filmmaker's perspective, they'd only amount to a first draft of the edit. Cutting a film is delicate balancing act, where scenes/shots that work well independently are often removed to service the pacing and flow of the larger narrative. There's no filmmaker in the history of cinema that's achieved a final cut of their movie straight out of the gate without going back for revisions. So, as much as Warriors Journey was billed as being "Bruce Lee's vision", it more accurately falls into the category of a work in progress. For me, though, Game of Death deserves to be more than just that.

RB: There are some strangely fascinating moments in Game of Death like when Bruce licks the top of his Nunchakus and then later licks his thumbs as he fights Kareem. Was Bruce just having fun or was he teasing his adversaries?

AC: There's a genuine cheekiness to Hai Tien that differentiates him from Lee's other screen characters. His mannerisms provided me with a good basis to write a full back story that justified his attitude. Essentially, he's a bloke who's spent the last decade of his life living in the public eye and building a distinct persona to manage his relationship with the outside world. This identity also extends to his approach to combat, whereby he employs tactics that physically, and psychologically, exploit his opponent's weakness. This has served him well in his fighting career and the moments you reference point to that. In terms of specifics... a male actor licking the base of a nunchuck stick under normal circumstances would be career suicide (laughter). In Lee's hands, it comes across as the epitome of cool — less erotic and more of an implied intimacy with his weapon; an 'I know something you don't' wink at his opponent. The overtone is pushed further with his gestures to Jabbar. As with his approach to the war cries, I believe Bruce was experimenting and towing the line between reality and hyper-reality to see just how much he could get away with on screen.

RB: Do you think as a filmmaker, you can bring more to the final footage, in terms of turning it from an end reel of an unfinished movie and more into a self-contained piece of standalone art?

AC: I believe so. Redux certainly feels complete to me, from the perspective of a story within a story. By the same token, it uses the trappings of action cinema to tell a deeper narrative that challenges the viewer with questions that don't necessarily have easy answers. Game of Death is an arthouse film that masquerades as a Kung Fu movie, though it's yet to be recognized as such by its fanbase.

RB: At the time of going to print only a few will have seen your "Game of Death Redux 2.0". Can you tell the reader if you think that the message in your new version is what Bruce was trying to convey in the footage that he shot?

AC: The pagoda sequence, at its core, is an exploration of the inner workings of the human psyche and how it relates to the physical and spiritual evolution of an individual. I feel that Redux is indicative of the direction Bruce was headed with his films. Whether he'd have made the same choices as me in terms of how he told the story is unknowable and ultimately irrelevant. What's important is that Lee's approach to the subtext in the action is front and center in my adaptation.

RB: Any works that have been recreated as a vision of what Game of Death might have looked like with the extra footage that has been made available in recent years (often fan edits) do not capture the true essence of what Bruce Lee was

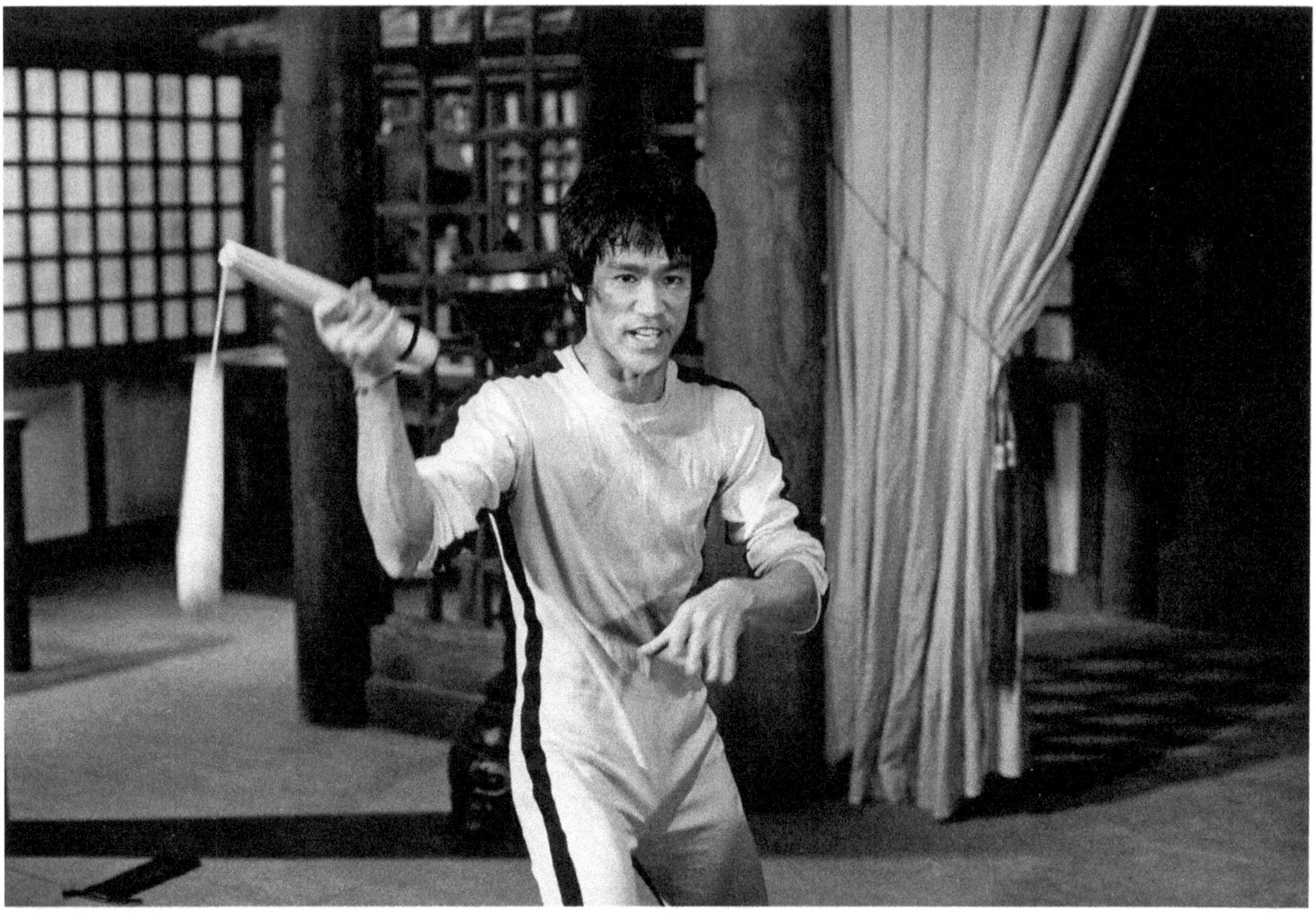

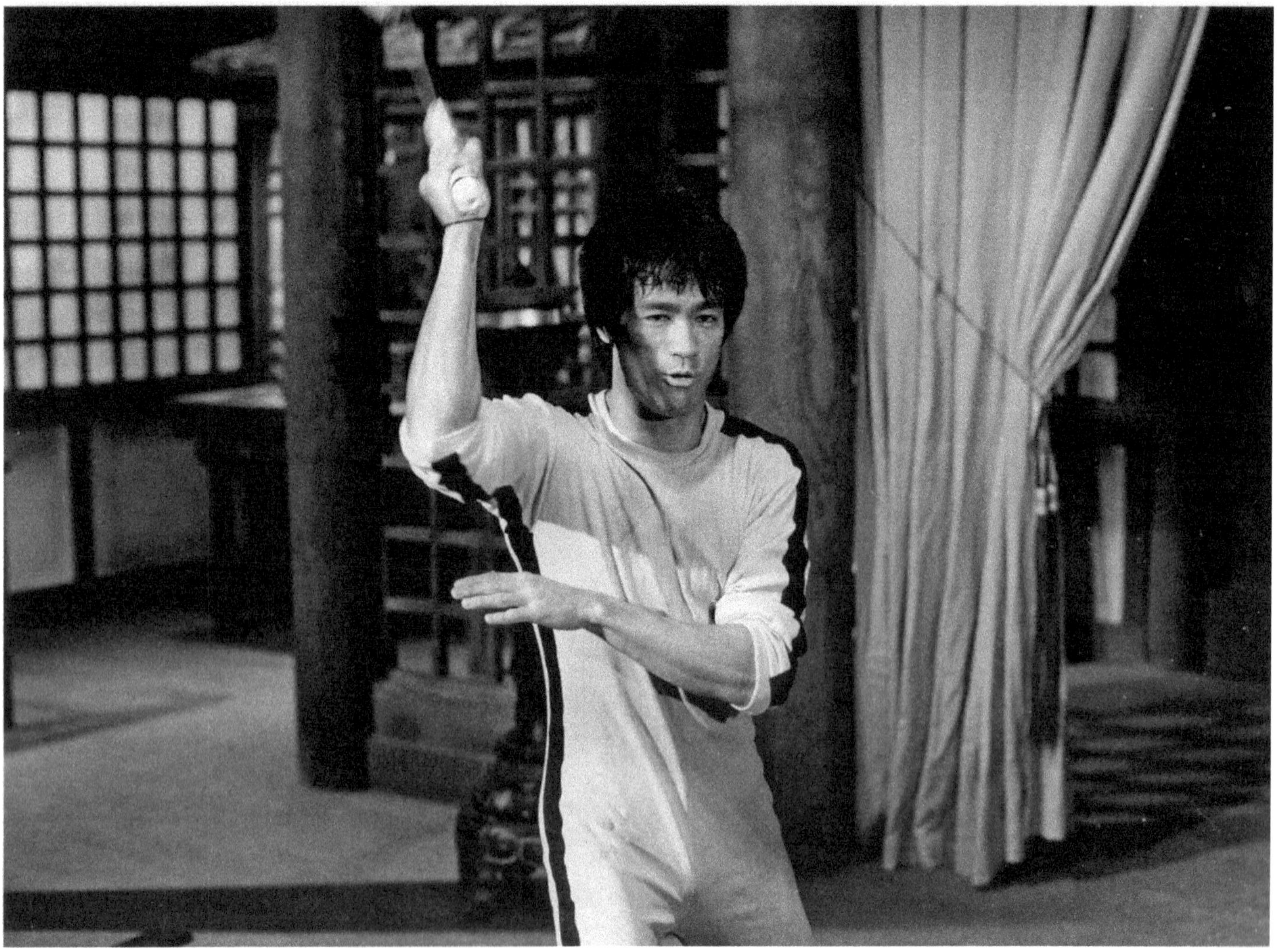

trying to achieve. Do you feel that your vision as a filmmaker, verses Bruce Lee's vision have a mutual understanding in a sympatico way?

AC: It's funny you ask this as a friend of mine recently noted that if Bruce and I had worked together on Game of Death, we'd have been at each other's throats the entire time (laughter.) And to be fair, there's truth in the statement. The answer to your question is contingent on a few variables. If we're referring to a complete full-length feature film, pre-Enter the Dragon, then, undoubtedly, our visions would diverge in the execution of the narrative. I think my sensibilities as a filmmaker are different from what Lee's were in the early 1970's. At the same time, I came up in an era that spawned some incredible filmmakers who shaped my entire perception of cinema and whose work Bruce never had the opportunity to see (and would surely have influenced him.) That said, I think we'd have found common ground in our respective approaches. I'd like to believe that Bruce would see merit in Redux.

RB: An interesting point is that in Bruce lee's notes he refers to the pagoda as "The Temple of the Leopard". What is your in24terpretation of this?

AC: I address this in my screenplay. It's a direct reference to the leopards that dwell in the mountains surrounding the pagoda. In folklore, they were seen as the primordial guardians of the temple.

RB: You have been kind enough to give Eastern Heroes some exclusive pages from your screenplay. Now that must have taken up some time. What inspired you to write a full screen play?

AC: It was really a consequence of giving the main characters a back story in order to fully understand their motives. As I began to decipher their history, it just snowballed, and I ended up running with it. I enjoyed the challenge of taking an outline that wasn't as good as its third act and giving it a level of depth that was consistent with the pagoda sequence.

RB: So, my next question is, will we see this published in the future, maybe as a companion when it gets a Blu-Ray release?

AC: It's been discussed, but it would have to be something worthwhile — otherwise, what's the point? There's one avenue I could see as a potential platform. Stay tuned.

RB: I was once in a conversation with someone who spoke to Unicorn Chan who had said the reason that the tracksuit was yellow was more because Bruce liked bananas. We may laugh but, being serious, what is your take on the yellow tracksuit?

AC: Going forward, I'll default to that explanation in future chats (laughter). All kidding aside, Bruce chose that colour scheme to reflect the colours of a tiger. Hai Tien's fighting moniker is, after all, the Yellow Faced Tiger. Mystery solved, hopefully. Beyond that, the tracksuit also reinforces Hai Tien as Lee's most Western character.

RB: Bruce Lee when interviewed about Game of Death said: "At present I am working on a script for my next film. I haven't really decided on the title yet, but what I want to show is the necessity to adapt one-self to changing circumstances. The inability to adapt brings destruction. I already have the first scene in my mind." How much of his original idea influenced you when working on Redux?

AC: I used Bruce's original outline as the basis for my screenplay. While there are elements of JKD peppered throughout the script, the central focus is really the metaphysical journey of a character who considers himself unbeatable — or, more accurately, would like to think he's unbeatable. The film's title is also very significant. On the surface it references the physical danger of the mission, but metaphorically it refers to the death of the ego whereby a spiritual transformation occurs that involves the death of the old self and the birth of the true self. During this process, commonly known as the dark night of the soul, an individual undergoes a difficult trial and becomes aware of a deeper perception of life. This newfound awareness is accompanied by the shedding of previous conceptual frameworks such as an identity, relationship, career or belief system that previously allowed the individual to construct meaning in their world.

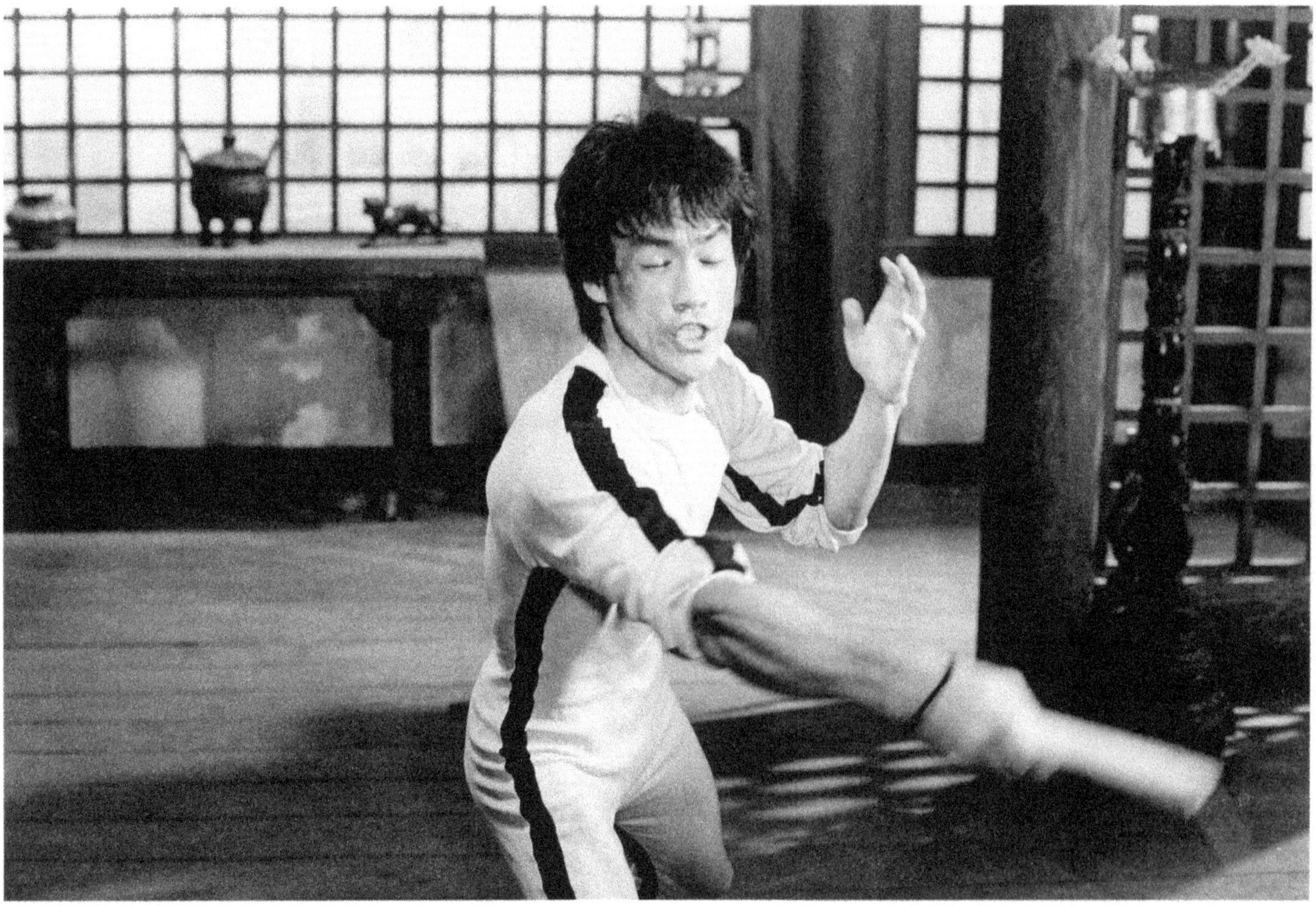

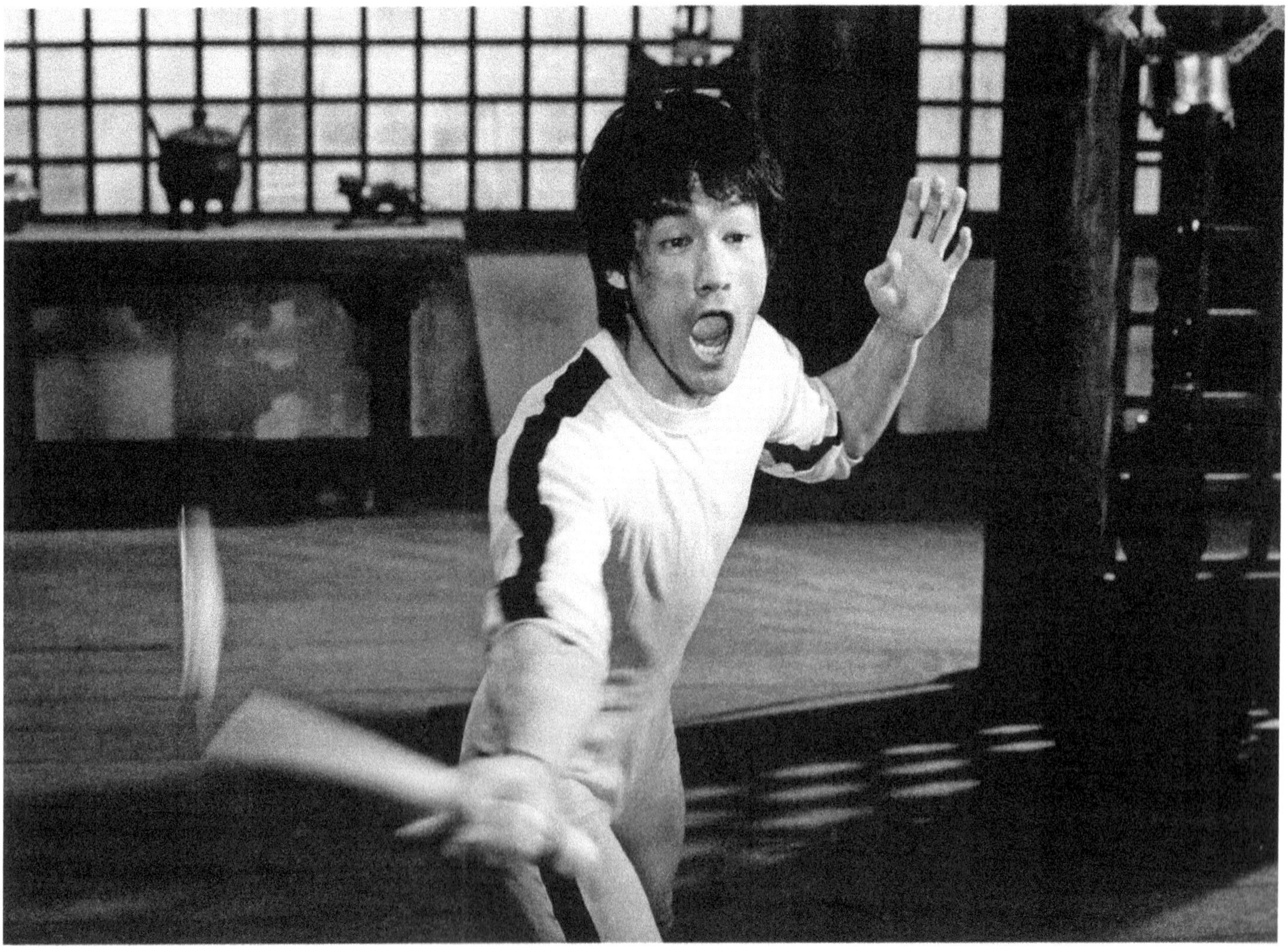

AC: In comparative mythology, ego death is described as "complete transcendence — beyond words, beyond space time, beyond self. There are no visions, no sense of self, no thoughts. There are only pure awareness and ecstatic freedom." Sound familiar? (laughter). It's the JKD mission statement.

RB: You talk about the Guardians representing aspects of Hai Tien. I would be interested to know how Dan Inosanto fits into this.

AC: Dan's floor is the Hall of the Tiger. His character, Pasquale, assumes the role of the Tiger, which corresponds with Hai Tien's fighting moniker in the story. As with Kareem, this suggests a thematic link between the two characters. There's a cockiness to Pasquale that's not unlike Hai Tien and I tend to view him as a less evolved version of Hai, or what Hai may have been prior to his combative evolution. On a subliminal level, they become figurative doppelgangers in the way they replicate each other's movements during the nunchaku portion of the battle. Perhaps most revealing is the way Hai Tien defeats Pasquale both physically and psychologically — whipping the Escrima master by taunting and mocking him in combat.

RB: What are your thoughts on Bruce's decision to use a pagoda in Game of Death as apparently, he had reportedly become enamored with the concept of using a Pagoda sequence while scouting locations for an earlier movie project, The Silent Flute in the early 1970's in Goa and Nepal?

AC: A little-known fact is that Lee initially conceived of the Game of Death idea when he was a teenager. In the early 1960's, he shared the concept of the story with his then girlfriend Amy Sanbo even as it continued to gestate in his mind for over a decade. It was partially inspired by the Twelve Labors of Heracles, a series of episodes in Greek mythology which chronicle Hercules performing seemingly impossible tasks across the world. I think the motif of ascending a tower lends itself to the idea of individualism and allegorically represents what we, as individuals, strive to do in life — reach the next level to hopefully become wiser versions of ourselves. Much has been written about action films being a form of escapism, and while there's an element of truth in that, I believe that at their best, they intrinsically connect audiences to hopes and fears that are vital to us as a species. Lee inherently understood this as a storyteller.

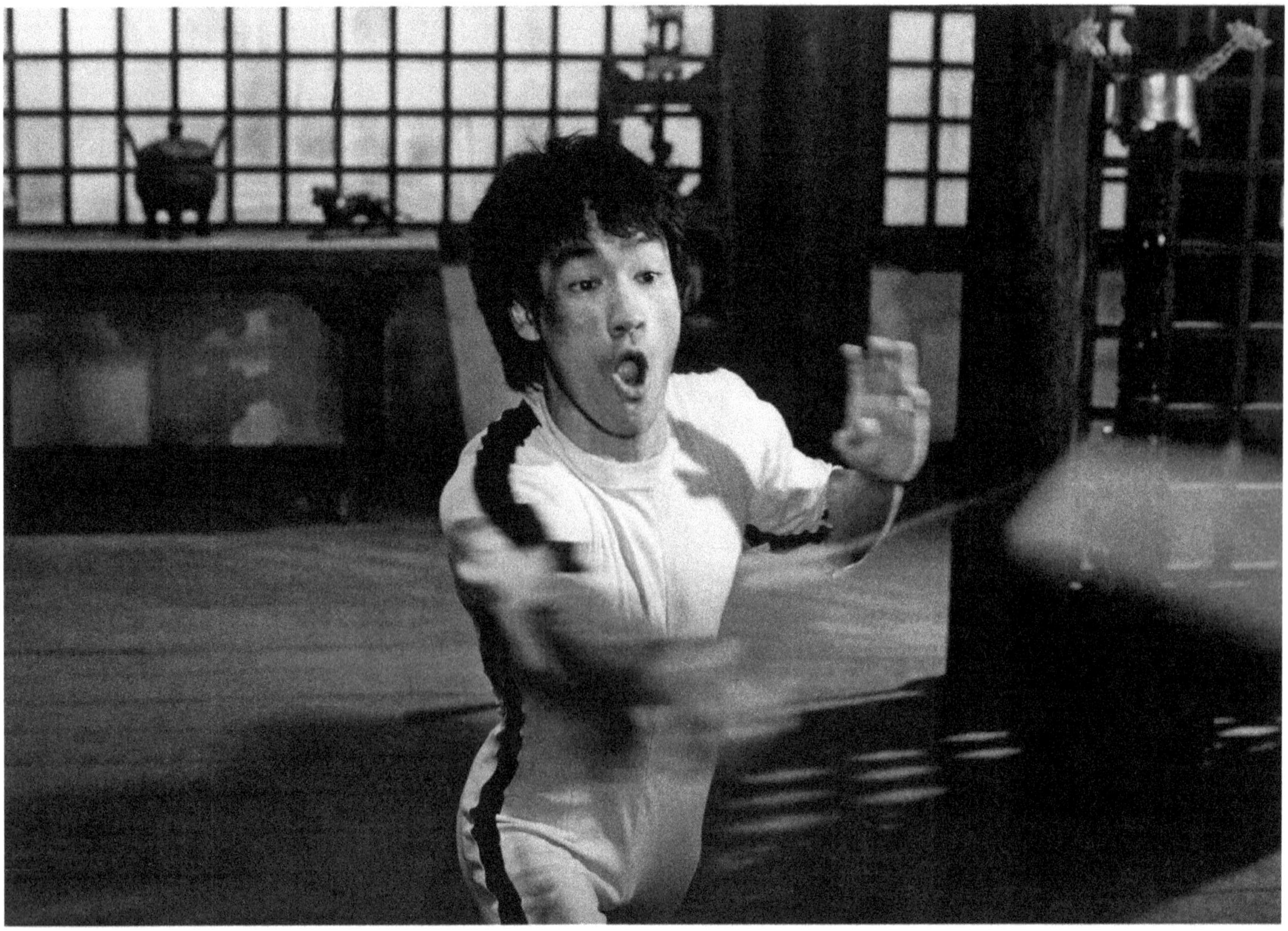

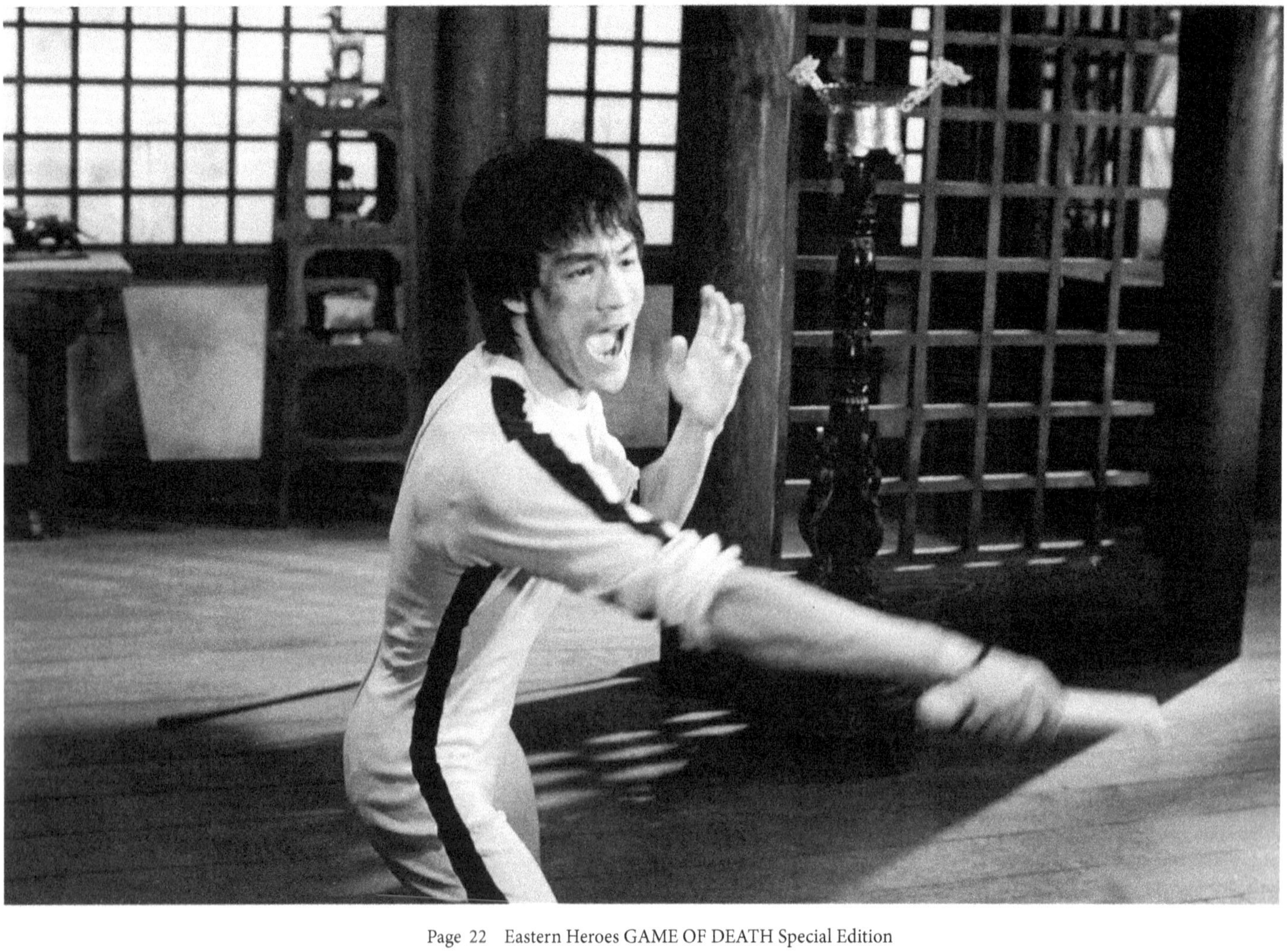

RB: Bruce Lee once said that he wanted his on-screen performances to be recognized as art! Do you feel that Redux 2.0 will demonstrate this in a more apparent way, as your version now takes this from what was once perceived as the end fight reels of an uncompleted film, to a more contained complete short movie that shifts it into the realm of arthouse?

AC: To me, Bruce's cinematic performances reflect the Zen proverb that suggests the highest art as the triumph over loss of art. Of course, art is highly subjective. The early 20th Century French novelist Marcel Proust said: "The real voyage of discovery consists not in seeking new landscapes, but in having new eyes." Redux is analogous to a violent ballet, where the subtext and emotion are expressed through simulated combat, rather than dance.

RB: Do you now see your finished edit as reaching a different audience outside of the Bruce Lee community, because it seems to now be more suitable to be categorized as standalone thirty-minute arthouse feature that would fit perfectly at the BFI in London?

AC: Absolutely. Game of Death has a built-in audience by virtue of the fact that it's a Bruce Lee piece. Redux's audience, though, are, first and foremost, cinema enthusiasts and storytellers. It's only with that crowd that Lee's art can break away from the lowbrow stigma connected with martial art films.

RB: Bruce Lee's original concept for Game of Death was to attempt to educate the movie audience. Creating awareness of different types of Martial Art and the advantages each of these may have in certain environments and situations. Game of Death would have been Bruce's second outing as a director, do you think having completed Way of the Dragon he was now a much more competent Director, and his original script would have made it a much better film?

AC: Great question. While Bruce's directing skills improved significantly from Way of the Dragon to Game of Death, much of it was relegated to the realm of action choreography. He was still a novice when it came to directing non-action sequences. The dialogue in his scripts needed work, which is apparent throughout the original Game of Death outline. My feeling is that, had Bruce completed Game of Death in 1972, the result would have been a mixed bag. I'm almost certain that the pagoda sequence would be the only portion of the film that would be truly revered by today's audience. His vision for the rest of the film was not as clear, and what little back story existed seems to have been just a means to an end.

RB: Let's assume for one moment that Bruce lee had lived. Do you think that the movie would have benefited from a second director to shoot the drama, leaving Bruce to direct the fight scenes that would appear in the last 50 minutes of the movie?

AC: I do, and, supposedly, there was talk of that happening. I haven't been able to verify whether this is true, but it was reported that Lee was interested in tapping Walter Chung Chang-Hwa, of King Boxer aka Five Fingers of Death fame, to co-direct Game of Death. If so, this would have given him the opportunity to entrust the non-action material to a seasoned filmmaker who potentially could've elevated the rest of the narrative to the same standard as the fight choreography.

RB: How much do you think Bruce observed and learned from Robert Clouse, that he would have utilized in his next film being this was Lee's first time working with a notable Hollywood Director?

AC: A shitload and, as a result, Game of Death would have been a completely different animal if he'd shot in 1973. I'm bewildered by Bruce Lee fans who continuously knock Robert Clouse's directorial skills. They often cite the segment in Enter the Dragon's underground cavern fight scene where Lee disposes of Han's henchman by the elevator doors. The consensus seems to be that Clouse didn't know how to shoot action because he framed the battle in a medium shot, rather than a long shot, leaving audiences unable to see the full choreography of the fight. What's lost on these critics is why Clouse chose to have Lee fight his way towards the camera while hitting his opponents outside of the frame. They have no awareness of the dramatic elements in that moment which are entirely expressed through Lee's body language. Like ballet, his every muscle movement in that shot conveys the character's emotional and psychological state during the battle. It's a perfect example of brilliant storytelling through action. Bruce used a similar cinematic technique with the killing of Kareem's character in Game of Death, framing the combat in a tight shot and having the camera slowly track from his face through the sofa panel before settling on the back of Kareem's hand gripping the sofa cushion. To me, that shot stands out as one of the most beautifully composed visuals in the history of cinema.

RB: Robert Clouse has received a lot of negative feedback both by the critics and Bruce Lee fans, and to be brutally honest I was amongst that number back in the day! Luckily over the years I've had many conversations with filmmakers that have helped educate me in recognizing how good a job Clouse did. In fairness, he had a massive challenge on his hands when he took the job to helm Enter the Dragon. Firstly, this was the first ever big budget martial arts movie. He was working with an Asian lead that had very little recognition outside of Hong Kong. And capturing Bruce Lee's art would have meant the framing and of the fight scenes would need to be just right in order to capture Bruce lee's speed and on-screen presence. I guess the biggest testament to Robert would be that the film is now coming up for its 50th anniversary and continues to be released on every new format and playing to the next generation of Bruce Lee fans. Can you give me another example of Clouse's storytelling that people would take note of next time the watched it?

AC: Another would be the sequence where Bruce visits his mother and sister's graves and looks over at the old woman sweeping the leaves. Her actions, framed in cut-away shots that appear closer with each glance, symbolically oversees Lee's character speaking to the two most important women in his life. If the scene had not played out that way, it wouldn't have been nearly as effective.

RB: As Game of Death was your cinematic introduction to Bruce, do you feel that if they had included the extra missing footage that this would have made a bigger impact on the 1978 movie? Or do you believe that the original cut with the omitted was the better route to take?

AC: That's a loaded question, because if they had used the full footage, I wouldn't be sitting here talking with you today (laughter). The reason Raymond Chow decided to eschew Bruce's original idea was due to the Bruceploitation market ripping off Lee's concepts and churning out a slew of movies that featured tracksuit wearing clones ascending various towers. Chow went a different direction and hired Bob Clouse to craft a loosely based biopic that centered around the last year of Lee's life. To justify the action, they played up the rumors of Bruce's involvement with Triads and his death being a result of foul play. By their estimation, this was a "fresh" take on the material and it fueled the hope that Lee, like the Billy Lo character, might still be alive. From a pure marketing and financial standpoint, it succeeded. In terms of Clouse's approach to the 1972 footage, the view seemed to be that James Tien and Chieh Yuan were appendages that weighed Bruce's fights down. So, they cut out the co-stars even at the expense of losing some great Lee moments from the footage. What I find amusing though, is how, at one point in the film, Billy's Uncle offers to put him in touch with "some men who can help" him against the syndicate. That may very well have been Clouse's consolation prize to Tien and Yuan (laughter).

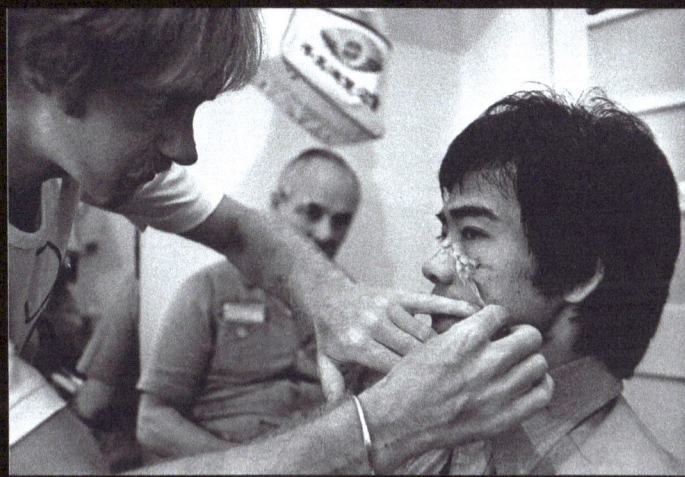

RB: Yeah, that would have been the perfect excuse to use the full footage.

AC: The most perplexing aspect of Game of Death 1978 though is the inconsistency around Billy's facial surgery. The dialogue suggests Billy needed time to 'get used to himself' due to the facial scarring from the bullet that fractured his face. Suspiciously, the scars have disappeared by the time we get to the 1972 footage in the finale. Logically, it would have made more sense if they just let Billy have his own look for the first half of the film and then pass off the difference in appearance to Bruce Lee as a post-surgery face change. But then we wouldn't have the awesome opening credits that reimagine Way of the Dragon's Coliseum battle.

RB: Do you think that there was any truth that he was going to bring Betty Ting Pei as a romantic lead for Game of Death I believe he also had told her she would be in Enter the Dragon but obviously he had second thoughts and maybe the offering of these parts where in passing chat?

AC: It's my opinion that he had no intention of including Betty in either Enter the Dragon or Game of Death. Whether he'd have cast her in a future project is anyone's guess, but, clearly, Bruce compartmentalized certain aspects of his life — his affair with Ms. Ting Pei being one of them.

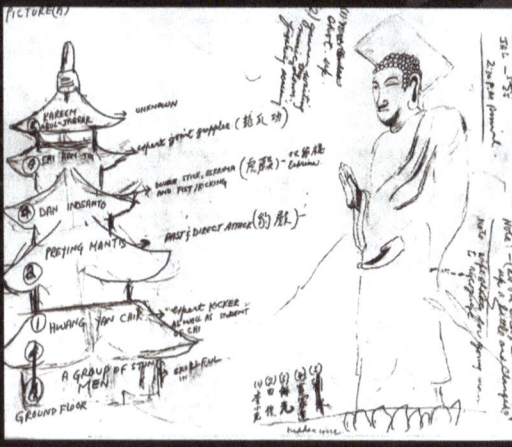

RB: One of the interesting points about Game of Death Redux is how you managed to discover the missing dialogue on Inosanto's floor?

AC: Thanks for acknowledging that, Ricky. I contracted multiple lip readers for

the job, so I was thrilled when they all came back with matching words. Fortunately, there were no discrepancies and, as these things often go, after the dialogue was deciphered, it all seemed so obvious (laughter). All kidding aside, they did an outstanding job. A lesser-known fact is I also had them take a stab at the alternate take from the dailies, where Bruce speaks a different line of dialogue. Unfortunately, due to the poor resolution of the footage, they were unable to decipher his lip movements well enough to give an accurate description of what was said. Still plagues me to this day.

RB: So, what were your reasons on deciding to excise portions of the dialogue and Hai Tien's thought narration on Kareem's floor?

AC: The golden rule of cinema is 'show don't tell.' Lee himself was aware of keeping dialogue to a minimum and emphasized the word motion in the phrase 'motion picture.' Kurosawa was a master of relaying an entire narrative through action, with very little dialogue spoken. While there are exceptions to the rule — the cinema of Quentin Tarantino and David Mamet come to mind — by and large many movies are overly expository. I got rid of Hai Tien and Jabbar's thought narration because cinema is at its best when performers are allowed to play the subtext in a narrative rather than spelling it out with dialogue. The narration was redundant because their thoughts were communicated perfectly through their body language during the fight. I didn't use Kareem's back and forth dialogue with Bruce, because Jabbar's character comes across as much more powerful and menacing as a silent figure. Those that cite Lee's notes as evidence of his plans to include all the dialogue have no understanding of the filmmaking process. Directors often write lines of dialogue and shoot scenes for coverage (to cover their bases) only to abandon them in post-production because the material didn't end up working the way they envisioned it. Bruce Lee would not have been immune to this. If you look at his other films, rarely do his characters speak during combat. Rather, they rely on their physicality to tell the audiences who they are and what they're feeling. Had Lee completed Game of Death, there's no doubt in my mind that he'd have cut some of the dialogue to serve a more cohesive story.

RB: We have two excellent Redux posters, a banner and debuting a third poster to feature in this book. Did you design these, or did you work with a Graphic Artist?

AC: I picked the images, but my buddy Darrin Stripe is the one who created the layout and colour scheme. I can't say enough good things about Dal and I give him full credit for how beautiful the posters turned out. He truly captured the arthouse aesthetic I was going for. Darrin also hosts a "Bruce Lee Movies" page on Facebook — which showcases alternate posters that he's done for Lee's other films — that I highly recommend checking out. I have to say that we were both surprised to discover how little the Game of Death promo photographs lend themselves to a good poster. The new one sheet I'm debuting for Eastern Heroes uses an image I've loved since I was ten years old — much gratitude to you, Ricky, for providing me with a high-resolution scan of the picture. The original photo saw Bruce standing on an apple box to match James Tien's height!

RB: My pleasure! I was recently talking to Toby Russell, and we discussed what direction Bruce's career might have taken if he had lived. Like you, we believe that Game of Death would have been scrapped or reshot with a bigger, better budget. When you and I spoke recently we agreed that Bruce was primarily an actor first, that used martial arts to gain recognition?

AC: Oh yeah, for sure. One thing that people tend to overlook is just how much of an anomaly Bruce Lee was to the world of cinema. In fact, there's never been quite a movie star like him. As a youth, Bruce's two primary outlets for performing were acting and dancing. Later he would bring the aesthetic he cultivated from those two disciplines to his

fight choreography. So, really, much of what made his screen combat so unique was fueled by artistic sensibilities — both as an actor and choreographer — equal to, if not more so, than his martial art skills. And though he may have liked to believe he was a martial artist first and an actor second, evidence suggests otherwise.

RB: I think you might lose a bit of love from the JKD crew (laughter)!

AC: They love me. It's important to remember that Bruce initially became passionate about martial arts for one purpose: to learn how to defend himself. In the beginning, it was a personal hobby that was not tied to his career aspirations. When he first arrived in the US, there were no immediate opportunities for him to pursue his acting goals, so he settled for teaching combat to a handful of guys that were enamored with his skills. It beat waiting tables. What it gave him though — besides developing his proficiency against some genuinely tough guys— was the opportunity to perform in front of crowds and effectively create the role of a young, precocious Gung Fu master. This gave him the prestige and attention he craved, but, more importantly, a platform to create the "Bruce Lee" persona that he would later impress his most devout Hollywood students and diehard fans with. It's worth noting that at no time during his twelve-year period in the States did he ever lose his passion for performing. So, from a historical perspective, his is a unique case of a performer who was devoted to a hobby (martial arts) which he then married to his dramatic impulses to become a genuine movie star. In doing this, he created a cinematic archetype — something no other film actor has ever achieved.

RB: What about movie stars like Stallone and Eastwood? Do you regard them as cinematic archetypes?

AC: Stallone and Eastwood embody two American archetypes in cinema that predate their careers in film. The difference with Lee is he created a specific movie hero that the world had not seen. It was a double-edged sword though because it typed him as an actor and, in the years that followed, it would have taken a considerable effort for him to break out of that mold. The fact that there's never been another actor in history who's had an entire film genre posthumously dedicated to his image speaks of the power of that archetype.

RB: Do you think that once he achieved fame with Enter the Dragon, he would have gone on to do more straight acting roles in Drama, Romance and Comedy?

AC: Yes, but again, it would have been an uphill battle. For example, Bruce was keenly aware of the difficulties he would face if he was cast in the role of a villain — particularly with his Asian audience. Marlowe was an anomaly in his filmography because he hadn't yet established the hero archetype. If you look at his acting career beyond the four films he made as an adult in Hong Kong, you'll see a wide range of roles that he played magnificently in his earlier years. I feel that he'd have eventually come to recognize the martial hero persona as his personal albatross.

RB: Where will people be able to see Game of Death Redux 2.0 when it releases?

AC: Currently, it's a race to see whether it lands on Blu-Ray or a streaming platform first. There's a possibility I may screen it in New York in the Fall. I'm also planning to do a limited-edition standalone Blu-Ray that will include a booklet, commentary and other cool extras. Currently, I'm in discussions, but it should be available sometime before the end of this year.

RB: As A filmmaker do you feel that you have breathed new life into the final sequence that you have created with Redux 2.0?

AC: When I first began this odyssey in December of 2018, my objective was to create a version of Game of Death that personally spoke to me. It was a passion project that drove me in every way because I couldn't bear the thought of the footage continuing to exist as anything less than the sum of its parts. I cared way too much about the material to leave it as it had been for another two decades. And although my mission didn't involve fighting different martial stylists in a temple, it did present its own set of challenges. Not surprisingly, one of them involved learning to let go of some of the preconceived notions I was accustomed to in the previous presentations of the edit. Another was being able to adapt to the technical confines of the source footage, which, was equally limiting and liberating in the process of restoring the film. It was an intense three years that was simultaneously fun, educational, joyful and frustrating. And it was a huge learning curve for myself and the amazing team I worked with — all of whom were instrumental in getting Redux where it needed to be. As I sit here today, having survived the game, I feel that I've achieved my goal. Of course, I recognize the finality in my statement which makes the experience all the more bittersweet. I'm deeply grateful for this period in my life which not only helped me grow as an artist but gave me the incredible opportunity to write a personal love letter to my childhood hero.

"Art is an affirmation of life, a rebuttal of death. And here we blunder into paradox again, for during the creation of any form of art, art which affirms the value and the holiness of life, the artist must die. To serve a work of art, great or small, is to die, to die to self

Filmaker Alan Canvan paying his respect at Bruce Lee's grave

Lake View Cemetary
Seattle, Washington
United States

Voicing the Game

With Alan Canvan and Chris Kent

AC: Chris, Game of Death was my very first Bruce Lee film. My first experience of him on screen was tied to war cries that, unbeknownst to me at the time, were dubbed by you for the 1978 feature-film. In addition to that, Lee only appears in about 25% of the movie. It was a helluva way to meet my hero for the first time(laughter). When did you first hear about Bruce Lee and which of his films did you see first?

CK: My first exposure to Bruce Lee was when I was an eleven-year-old kid and I saw The Green Hornet television show. That was when martial arts struck a resonant chord inside me. The first Bruce Lee film I saw was Enter the Dragon, which premiered shortly after I began training in Jeet Kune Do under Dan Inosanto in his backyard gym in Carson, California.

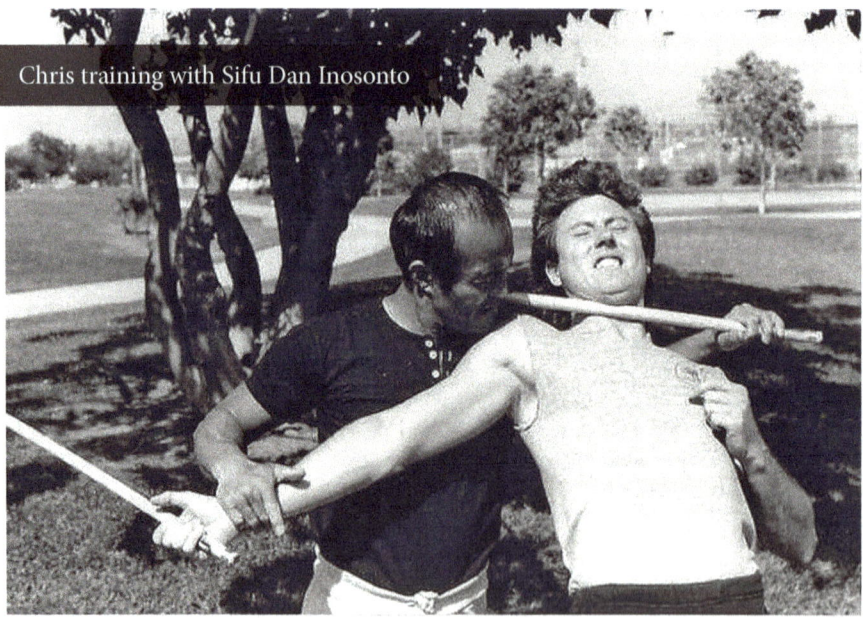

Chris training with Sifu Dan Inosonto

AC: Tell me how you got involved with the 1978 movie.

CK: I had been training under my instructor, Sifu Dan Inosanto, for about five years at the time. He had recently returned from Hong Kong where he had been involved in the completion of Bruce Lee's unfinished film, Game of Death. He had also just finished looping some voiceover material for his action scenes at Columbia Studios and told me that they were looking for someone to do Bruce's war cries and yells. I had been messing around doing it for a few years, and Dan said to me, "I know, you can do it." I had never done that sort of thing before, but Dan said, "Come with me." We went into his garage, and he ran a small 8mm film of some of the fight scenes which had been shot by someone sitting in the Sing Lee movie theater in Chinatown. Then he started coaching me as we watched it over and over, telling me, "Now do this…now yell that," etc. So, we did this for about an hour. Then Dan arranged for me to meet the producers at the studio, and I had to do an audition for them in a sound studio while watching some of the fight action. At the end of the audition, they told me I had the job. So, I spent two full days at the studio, watching all of the fight scenes, including the ones using a stand-in for Bruce, over and over again and yelling and screaming my head off. It was hard work but a helluva lot of fun. I was paid for my work but didn't receive any type of screen credit.

AC: You did such an amazing job that, for years, I believed the battle cries were Bruce's real voice. Did the 8mm reel you saw in Dan's garage contain fight scenes from Game of Death?

CK: Yes, the 8mm film of clips of Game of Death I watched in Dan's garage was shot by someone at the Sing Lee movie theatre in Los Angeles Chinatown.

AC: As I was putting together the audio for my first iteration of Game of Death Redux, I tried to use as much of your voice as possible because, not only was the tone right, but the dubs accurately reflected Bruce's lip movements and expressions much more so than his actual war cries that were slapped on to the previous edits. My first version, which was released on the Criterion box set, used a combination of your voice and Bruce's, which I feel, in retrospect, was too much of a compromise. I was delighted when you agreed to work on my updated version. What was it like seeing Bruce's expressions synced to your voice the very first time?

CK: Kind of surreal… and extremely gratifying. It was really cool and an amazing experience. For me, it was an honor to be involved in a project that was Bruce Lee's. To have my voice linked with Bruce Lee's fight sequences in his film made me feel that I was in some small way sharing in his incredible martial legacy. And, I don't know, maybe honoring him somehow. And that was great. I worked really hard and felt I did the best work I was capable of. In addition to that, I got to see the edited version of Bruce's fight scenes before anyone else other than the producers and people had.

AC: Did the producers give you any direction during the sessions, or did they just let you do your thing?

CK: Basically, they let me do my own thing, because I don't think they were really sure of what they needed. They would give me technical advice at some points and request numerous retakes if they felt the sound didn't mesh with the film. But basically, I was on my own.

AC: Were you aware at the time of how much more footage there was compared to the eleven minutes we got in the 1978 film? What were your initial thoughts upon first seeing the footage and being a martial artist, where do you rank Game of Death in terms of Bruce's other fight choreography?

CK: I knew from what had been written about the film at the time that there was about an hour or so of film footage, some of which were outtakes and bloopers. I was excited to be one of the first people in the world to see the fight footage in depth, however I only saw the footage they chose to edit and include in the film. As someone else edited the film, you cannot really say it was Bruce's film, but I thought the choreography was great. Very dynamic and ahead of its time cinematically compared to anything else out there. The inclusion of the various weapons much more grappling in the film made it much more interesting as well.

AC: Did Dan Inosanto ever discuss the missing 'log scene' footage with you?

CK: He mentioned it briefly, and that he beats up the guy wearing the karate uniform and basically does the Kenpo "dance of death" on him. But that was it. It's kind of a shame that it disappeared and couldn't be used in the film.

AC: Did he give you any idea of how long the sequence ran, or where it might possibly be today?

CK: The answer is no to both questions. He had no clue what had happened to the footage.

AC: How about the outdoor filming in the New Territories? The footage plays like a film 'reel' on the guardians for Bruce's character and his companions to review prior to the raid in the 1972 version?

CK: The only thing that Dan mentioned to me was that it was Bruce running through some fight choreography ideas for the film. That's why Bruce is wearing street clothes and not dressed in the one-piece tracksuit. One of the people who can be seen working with him in that footage was Wu Ngan, who had worked for the Lees for a few years as a servant.

AC: Many fans aren't aware that Changsha, the Rhythm Man character from the unproduced Silent Flute project was based on Inosanto. I always saw Dan's character in Game of Death as a slightly tweaked version of Changsha. Obviously, the character was meant to illustrate the peril of relying on martial patterns. There are parallels between his and Bruce's character though, both in how they mirror each other in the nunchaku duel as well as their respective monikers — Dan representing the Hall of the Tiger, and Bruce playing the role of the Yellow Faced Tiger. Did Dan ever mention this to you or give any additional details about his character (ie his background, name etc?)

CK: Dan just told me that his character was an Escrimador, and that Bruce wanted to include a great deal of the use of rhythm and broken rhythm in the action, and that Bruce wanted to illustrate certain ideas in the film, such as dealing with set patterns of action from his opponents. I found the Changsha character that appeared in The Silent Flute to be much different. From a discussion I had with the screenwriter Stirling Silliphant, Changsha the Rhythm Man was supposed to be a martial artist who could move rhythmically, draw his opponent into his rhythm, and then suddenly break that rhythm and destroy the opponent.

AC: Yeah, Lee essentially splits the character between Dan and himself in Game of Death. There were a lot of ideas that Bruce carried over from project to project from the period of 1969-1973. One thing that's rarely looked at is the nature of the primordial war-cries Lee developed for film and how, in many ways, they stood in for dialogue. Clearly, they stemmed from Bruce's dramatic roots and were completely unique to both him and cinema. They come across as both fierce and playful, containing their own implicit language, and communicating a range of emotions underneath the surface. Were you consciously aware of this when you approached your work on Game of Death, or was it more of just trying to ape his style and doing something you felt worked?

CK: It wasn't a thing about simply trying to mimic Bruce or doing things the audience would think are cool. I think I just tried to be honest with each scene and what each yell or cry dealt with. As you said, there are some moments where Bruce is super intense, others where he a bit more playful and not taking the opponent over-seriously. And times, like when he's

fighting Kareem Jabbar, where he gets pounded and then just turns around and comes back fighting like a wildcat. So how could I vary the tones and sounds for those different moments. Again, as I said, I'd never done anything like this and was learning on the fly, as they say.

AC: What are some of your favorite moments in the footage? Were there any portions that were more fun to dub? On the flip side, were there any parts that were particularly difficult?

CK: The actual fights between Bruce and Dan, Chi Han Jae and Kareem were definitely the most fun part, because it was Bruce! I'd have to say that I really liked the fight between Bruce and Ji Han Jae, the Hapkido expert. The most difficult parts were the weapon fight scenes because there is so much action going on and sometimes Bruce's face was covered by his arms.

AC: The reason Bruce's war cries in other films don't sync well with Game of Death, is that, in Game, he took a more amplified approach, with a mocking quality to his facial expressions that were more understated in his previous offerings. What's your take?

CK: Well, part of may have to do with the fact that when Bruce was making Game of Death, he had not been offered Enter the Dragon, and while he was now a big star in Hong Kong, he wasn't in the West. So, I think that at the time the film was being made primarily for Asian audiences, and there are different sensibilities between Western audiences and Asian audiences. I remember reading that Enter the Dragon was actually the least popular of Bruce Lee's films in Hong Kong because they felt it was too Western, although maybe that's changed now. I think back to what Bruce's wife, Linda, who is a close and dear friend, said about the film quite awhile ago, and that was that she felt that Game of Death was truly Bruce's baby, and that he wanted to really express himself fully in it. He was attempting to capture and convey different moods and emotions in fight action. So sometimes his looks are almost condescending of the opponent, and other times they show concern, and other times exasperation and possibly even a little fear. And I think the war cries work hand-in-hand to support that.

AC: What were your thoughts when I first contacted you and asked if you'd be interested in working on

my new versioof Redux?

CK: Oh man, I was excited and immediately taken with the idea. To be able to involved on the film again and do the same type of work after such a long time would be like seeing and spending time with an old friend again. And, as I said before, to share in Bruce's legacy and in some small way be a part of that… who wouldn't want to do that?

AC: In revisiting the footage after forty-three years, did you approach the material any differently than in 1977?

CK: I don't think so. Like the first time I worked on the film, I tried to get into Bruce's mindset, what feeling or emotion he was conveying or attempting to convey. What sort of sound would fit that moment. I guess we'll only know if I was successful when we see the finished result. I hope I was.

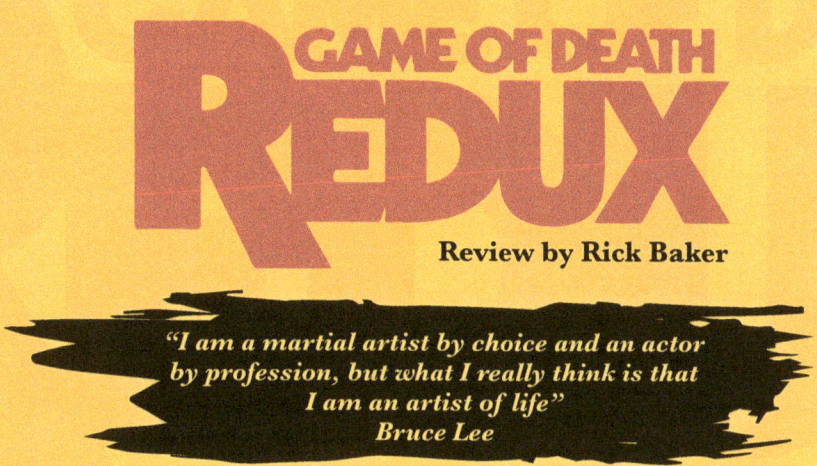

GAME OF DEATH REDUX

Review by Rick Baker

"I am a martial artist by choice and an actor by profession, but what I really think is that I am an artist of life"
Bruce Lee

I have always possessed an appreciation of Bruce Lee's unfinished Game of Death, dating back to my first viewing in 1978, when UK audiences were 'treated' to the most stripped-down version possible, thanks to the head of the BBFC, James Ferman, taking issue with the nunchaku scenes. Even though the worldwide release reinstated those drastic cuts that we suffered, there was still a great deal of footage that was omitted.

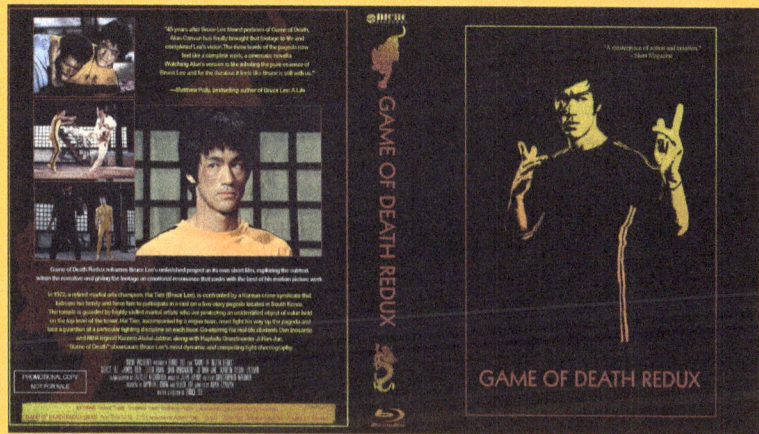

Redux Blu-Ray Promo Cover

In more recent years, the internet has proven to be a fruitful source for allowing the masses to see the missing scenes discovered by Bey Logan when he worked for Media Asia. Various fan edits have emerged, providing – in their view – a more 'complete' version of Lee's opus. One such edit came to my attention in 2019. I was having a discussion with my old friend, Alan Canvan. He informed me that he had put together his own version of the film, called Game of Death Redux. I was incredibly excited to see his vision. I asked him if he would like the opportunity to exclusively screen his version to an audience at the Kung Fu Café in Stratford, London. He kindly agreed,

Artport Version

Redux Version

and I was very excited to see his interpretation. Our optimism was justified - the audience, including myself, were very impressed with Alan's version. The cuts were excellent, and the edits provided a very fluid viewing experience. We even set up a video link at the end of the showing, so that the audience could ask Alan questions about his edit. I later discovered that the version we showed was actually a working print. Such was its positive reception, that it was included as an extra on the Bruce Lee Criterion boxset, although Alan has since confirmed that the version presented in Stratford was slightly longer. Let us jump forward to 2022. Once again, I was talking to Alan about his latest edit of the movie – Redux 2.0. When I first read about his updated version, I was intrigued. I was very keen to get back in touch with him, to glean more information about the changes he had made to enhance the film. I was very fortunate that Alan took the time to bring to my notice many facets and details about Game of Death to which I previously haven't paid a great deal of attention. This has provided me with a deeper level of understanding, and made

my viewing a much more complete experience. It has piqued my interest to ascend another floor of the pagoda. I have been fortunate over the years to spend time with many people who possess an excellent knowledge of Bruce Lee. The depth of their expertise, and their ability to discuss and debate every aspect of his films, has always resulted in a superior viewing experience for me. Alan's expertise has enabled me to reassess the film, and enjoy Game of Death in the same manner.

To anyone reading, I say this: read the interview between myself and Alan before you watch the film. It will enrich your experience immeasurably. Clear your mind of the previous times you have watched the movie. In its place, you will notice the time, effort and passion that Alan has invested in converting this end-of-reel sequence into a more complete piece of work. Every frame has been meticulously pored over, considered, and utilised in the best possible way. His dedication and love for the movie has created a self-contained 31-minute epic, depicting Bruce Lee's art at its best.

After our initial conversations, the time finally came for the viewing. I was more excited than I thought I would be. I was eager, with the knowledge I had acquired, to see this film from a new perspective. From the opening narrative by Alan, to Bruce Lee ascending the stairs, to the finale with him descending the stairs, I was absolutely transfixed. I didn't want to miss a frame. I wanted to give Alan my honest opinion about his new edit, and how it compared to the 2019 version, so I made sure that I viewed the movie through the prism of my newly-gained knowledge.

In a nutshell, it is a triumph. He has beautifully executed the editing, which enables the sequences to segue more organically than ever before. The colours have been enhanced where possible. The dubbing is vastly improved, and the war cries, rather than being stripped from an existing Bruce film, have been re-dubbed to create a more authentic sound. There is a real sense of context evident in his cries. The music cues are utilised incredibly well. Alan has built tension and used the music for dramatic effect throughout. Every scene is enhanced by his use of the soundtrack. I don't know whether or not we lavish enough praise on John Barry, but we should. His title score is magnificent, and its potential is realised fully in Redux 2.0.

Alan has presented this film from the perspective of a filmmaker. The only person to do that previously was Robert Clouse in 1978. There is a vast difference between a fan edit than that of a film makers cut. Unlike traditional film editing, which is characterized by a new assemblage of original film or video content, fan editing is a form of recombinant filmmaking that reactivates existing arrangements of audio-visual material. A film maker's Cut is a version of a movie that tries to match the director's original vision. Since most film Makers/ directors aren't given "final cut" privileges, it is the studio that dictates the version that gets released. A Director's Cut is typically released after the film has had an initial theatrical run. This "director-approved" version is typically released in the home video market. For "Game of Death Redux.2.0" Alan has approached this both as a film maker/and Director, to create a coherent self-contained short movie in its best possible form creating masterpiece of art-house cinema. Let's be realistic! No other Bruce Lee film has showcased him depicting his art, his acting and his directing, and not forgetting the way he frames a movie like we witness in G.O.D Redux.20. This has only been achieved now by the aesthetic eye and dedication of Alan.

This is in laymen's terms, means we get, as the viewer, almost 30 minutes of Continuous Bruce Lee demonstrating his art over three levels without very little interruption when engaging each challenge. In conversation with Alan we chatted about the end scene, were Bruce is strangling Kareem, and the way the Camera glides from Bruce's face through the sofa panel to Kareems hand. This shot alone is worthy of cinematic recognition, that would be duly noted by any cinema buff.

In Summery this is not Alan offering up what he believes to be Bruce Lee's vision. No! This is Alan taking the ingredients of what is available, and like a Michelin Chef turning it into visual experience, by plating up a magnificent effort, combining music and the on screen charisma of Bruce Lee and making it a much more palatable experience for the viewer.

I can only stress that if you read and digest the interview between me and Alan, it is to be hoped that some (not all) will appreciate this new viewing experience with out fast forwarding in search of some new footage. And the next generation of Bruce Lee fans will view this first and not be mind cluttered with what has gone before.

CHARACTER NOTES

CHARLIE WANG – Chinese, 31 years old. Local martial arts champion in Southeast Asia who never quite made the big time; Cunning and deceptive, known for his connection to Hong Kong Triads; Incredibly envious of Hai Tien's career and resents that Hai is co-leads the raid team under Chul's orders; Goes to great lengths to appear to be more than he is - smoke and mirrors all the way.

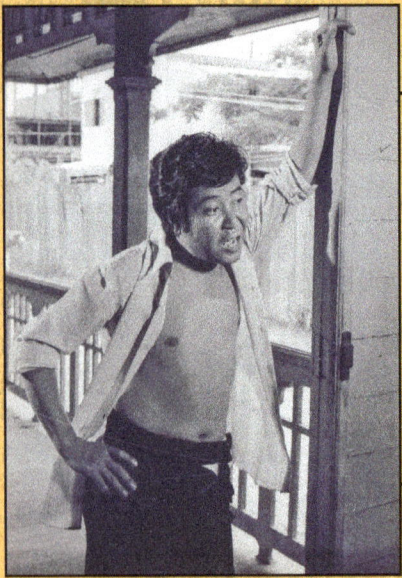

PANG MA – Chinese, 38 years old. A local petty thief and locksmith with a drinking problem hired for peanuts to unlock the treasure box. Or is he? Not much is known about Pang except that he's cheap and viewed as an annoying appendage to the others; More to him than meets the eye.

HAI TIEN LEUNG – Chinese American, 32 years old. Comes from Middle Class family that wavered between living in Hong Kong and Los Angeles before settling in San Diego when he was around eleven years old; Became the reigning lightweight martial arts champion of the world when he was twenty-four years old and has been defending his title seven years; An incredible fighter that's adored by millions with a level of fame is comparable to Sugar Ray Leonard in the early 80's; Recently retired, undefeated. This story will chronicle what matters most to him even as him as he walks a life path to understand who he truly is.

OH-SEONG – Korean, 33. Guardian to the Gate of Enlightenment. A Hapkido and Tae Kwon Do stylist who guards the entrance way of the pagoda; Leads a group of 20 Goju Karate men; His shins are so conditioned that he's been known to split birch trees with them.

PASQUALE – Filipino, 30. Guardian of the second-floor aka Hall of the Tiger. Escrima and Kenpo Stylist; Fierce and exceptionally proficient with blunt weapons and nunchaku; Rumored to have hunted and killed a Bengal Tiger with his bare hands.

© Copyright Alan Canvan 2022

UNKNOWN – Guardian of the fourth-floor aka Hall of the Unknown. Unorthodox style; Virtually no information exists on this fighter. Known to be incredibly formidable and dangerous; Only one individual, now clinically insane, has ever escaped his wrath; Reportedly cannibalistic, consuming his opponents; certain cultures refer to him as "Hakim" aka The Judge.

KANG-MIN – Korean/Chinese, 34. Guardian of the third-floor aka Hall of the Dragon. Hapkido and Dragon Claw Stylist; Considered untouchable having honed angular attacks with extraordinary grip strength; His maternal ancestry goes back to the Kangxi Emperor of the Qing Dynasty.

LAURA LEUNG – American, 31 years old. Hai Tien's wife of nine years, smart, beautiful and tough as nails; Very much in love with Hai – she's his rock, providing moral support and stability for her family since they've been together.

BILLY LEUNG – American, 7 years old. Hai Tien and Laura's son. A precocious youngster who, like most children that age, idolizes his Dad. He often spends time in his imaginary world and loves creating elaborate stories his toy action figures.

MR. CHUL – Korean. 58 years old. Head of one of the most powerful crime syndicates in Southeast Asia; Cunning and ruthless; A multi-millionaire who has monopoly over various legal and illegal businesses throughout Korea, Hong Kong and Taiwan. Though the Government and Authorities are aware of him, his prominence in the region, along with his political connections keep him from facing repercussions.

KINCAID – American, 34 years old. Ex-military mercenary; Former middle weight boxer; Having been on the battlefield, he's proficient, methodical and deadly. Of the entire team, physically the most capable, next to Hai Tien; Befriends Hai Tien in the days leading up to the raid.

NIU FENG – Chinese, 29 years old. Former bodybuilder and Olympic athlete; Quite strong but dimwitted, very much a bull in a China shop; Prideful and brash, extremely reactive to any situation; Accepts the mission because he enjoys combat and sees the mission as his path to glory.

HUANG CHIA DA – Chinese/Korean, 33 years old. A construction foreman who resides in Korea, originally from Beijing martial artist in Beijing; Known for his martial skills; Has come on hard times and accepts the mission because he needs a large sum of cash for an ailing family member's surgery.

SHUN YUAN – Chinese, 38. Guardian of the ground floor aka Hall of the Praying Mantis; Wing Chun and Praying Mantis Stylist who has a reputation for being the premier close quarter combat exponent of the world. His hand combinations are known to be incredibly fast and powerful.

GAME OF DEATH

A Screenplay by
Alan Canvan

EXCLUSIVE EXERTS FROM ALAN CANVAN'S GAME OF DEATH
© Copyright Alan Canvan 2022

SCREENPLAY BY :

"The way of the warrior is to be found in dying. Live as though already a corpse and you will find freedom." - Yamamoto Tsunetomo, Hagakure: The Book of the Samurai

FADE IN:

EXT. SOGNISAN MOUNTAINS, KOREA — DAWN

Open wide on a snow laden terrain in the middle of a heavy winter storm. A leopard leaps into the foreground chasing a hare. As they run off into the distance we track across the terrain to a giant oak tree.

O.S. the loud snap of a main branch falls under the weight of the heavy snow. We pull back and settle on a thin willow tree in the foreground, bending and surviving the harsh wind.

INT. GYM - DUSK

O.S. The sound of controlled breathing punctuated by the rhythmic sound of a speed bag rattling as we track across weights, heavy bags and the main boxing ring in the center of the gym before resting on a large standing mirror resting against the back wall. We move in on the reflection as a young man steps into frame, executing lightning fast strikes and kicks that make the air pop. This is HAI TIEN LEUNG, 30 years old, beautiful and the world's reigning Lightweight Martial Arts Champion. We linger on the reflection for a beat and DISSOLVE TO:

CREDIT SEQUENCE set to Led Zeppelin's" Ramble On": A colorful montage that documents Hai Tien's ascent to fame following his career and personal life through televised matches, newspaper headlines, magazines, talk shows and home movies. Towards the end of the montage we focus on a headline that announces his retirement as we

DISSOLVE TO:

INT. KAI TAK AIRPORT, HONG KONG - DAY

HAI TIEN, along with his wife, LAURA, and young son, BILLY, have just arrived from Los Angeles and await a layover to Tokyo in the airport's VIP lounge.

Hai is being interviewed by a local reporter for one of
Hong Kong's leading newspapers.

    REPORTER

You announced your plans to retire a few weeks ago. This
came as quite a shock to the sports world. What can we
expect next from you?

    HAI TIEN

A much-needed rest (laughter.) I have a few things up my
sleeve, but you'll have to wait to hear about them. For
now, I'm on hiatus, but I'll say this much - the next
chapter will be significant.

    REPORTER

You've been an ambassador for the Martial Arts and
popularized the sport all over the world. Will you continue
to represent it in the future?

    HAI TIEN

Well, the thing is, fighting is no longer a challenge to me.

    REPORTER

In what respect?

    HAI TIEN

In every respect. I mean, to tell you the truth, I can beat
anyone in the world.

EXT. CHUL'S ESTATE GROUNDS - DAY

The team trains in the open garden of Chul's estate. HAI
TIEN leans against a large tree, arms folded and observes
from a distance as CHARLIE WANG bosses the fighters as they
practice combat drills. Charlie leads Niu Feng to the side
away from the others.

    CHARLIE

You should be leading this team with me instead of that
paper tiger. Defeat him and Mr. Chul will promote you.

                    NIU FENG

Yes. I'll show him.

Niu Feng walks across the training area and approaches Hai Tien. He speaks in Cantonese.

                    NIU FENG

I challenge you.

                    HAI TIEN

Alright. First, let me show you something.

As he utters the last word Hai throws a back fist off of his folded arms - catching Niu on the bridge of the nose and knocking him down. Niu is out for about ten seconds then comes to, dazed and humiliated.

                    HAI TIEN

Combat is similar to music. A good musician plays the notes, but a great musician understands the space between them.

EXT. CHUL'S MANSION TERRACE - NIGHT

Hai Tien stands on the balcony, taking in the stars and evening air. Kincaid joins him on the terrace.

                    KINCAID

It ain't my business, but glad you accepted this mission.

                    HAI TIEN

Is that so?

                    KINCAID

Yeah, Chul knows I'd never take orders from Wang. I work alone mostly. Except when I don't

> HAI TIEN

Why'd you sign on then?

> KINCAID
>
> (beat)

I did a job in the Middle East a couple of years back. Ankara, Tunis, Cairo. Legend has it that man's greatest fear dwells in that temple. I'd be lyin' if I said I wasn't a little bit curious.

> (long beat)

The Bedouins believe that treasure holds the key to immortality. They call the guardian of the final floor Hakim. It means 'the Judge' in their language.

> HAI TIEN

You believe that?

> KINCAID

No. But...the game of death is as old as time itself. Many attempt the challenge, few survive. Cherokee warriors would often prepare their death song before battle, in case it was their day to cross over the great divide.

> HAI TIEN

Have you prepared yours?

> KINCAID

I've stared death in the face too many times to give a shit.

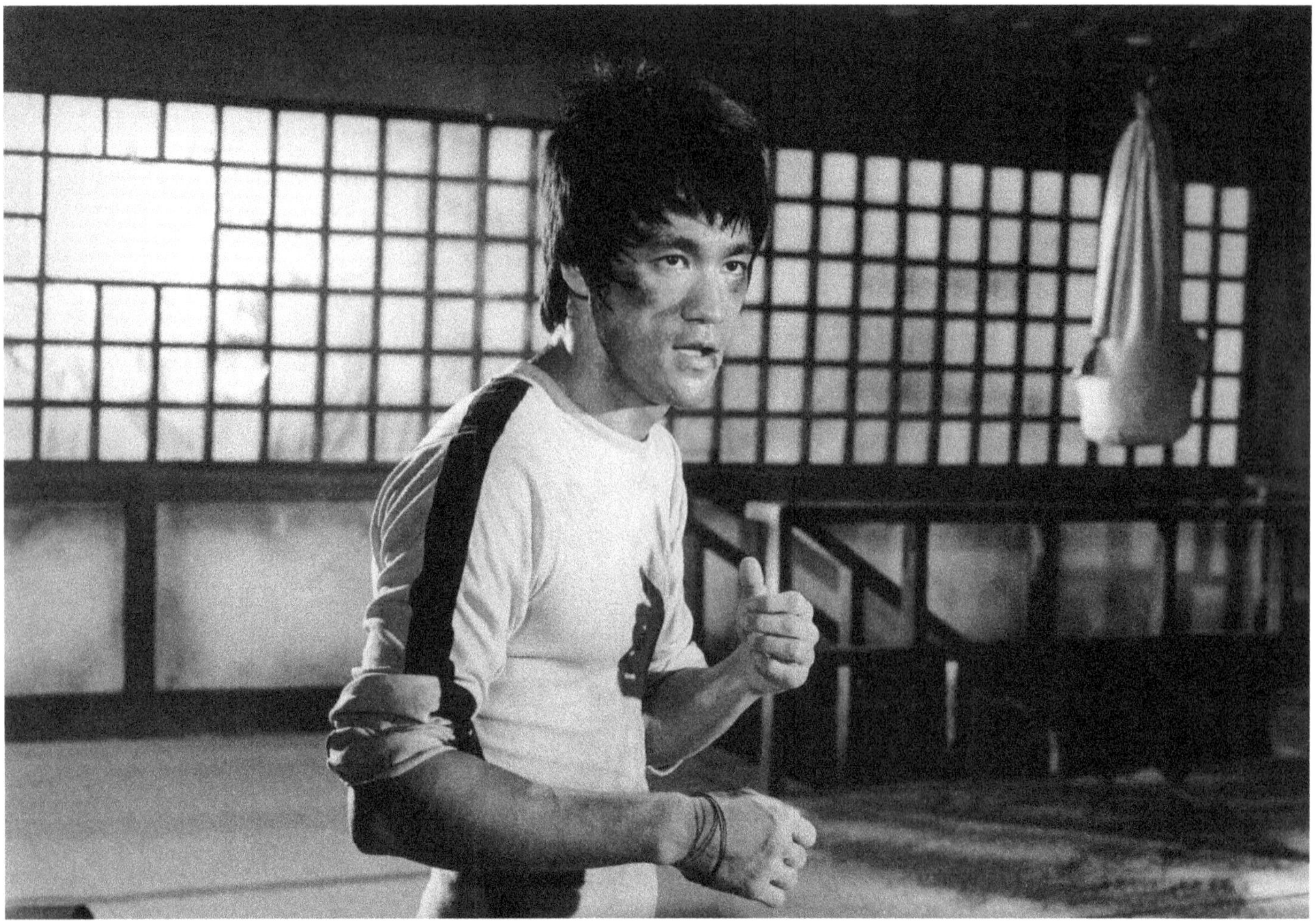

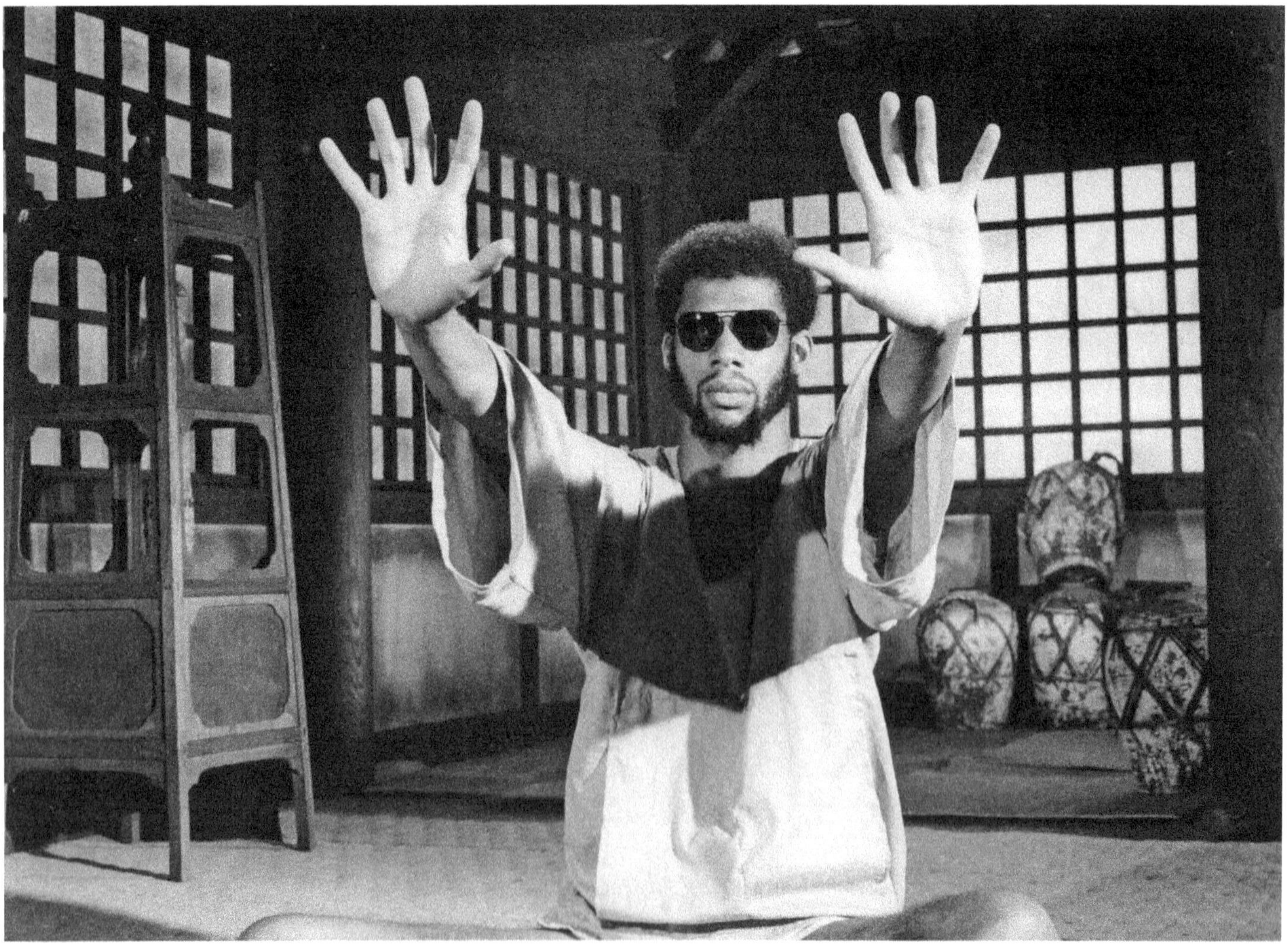

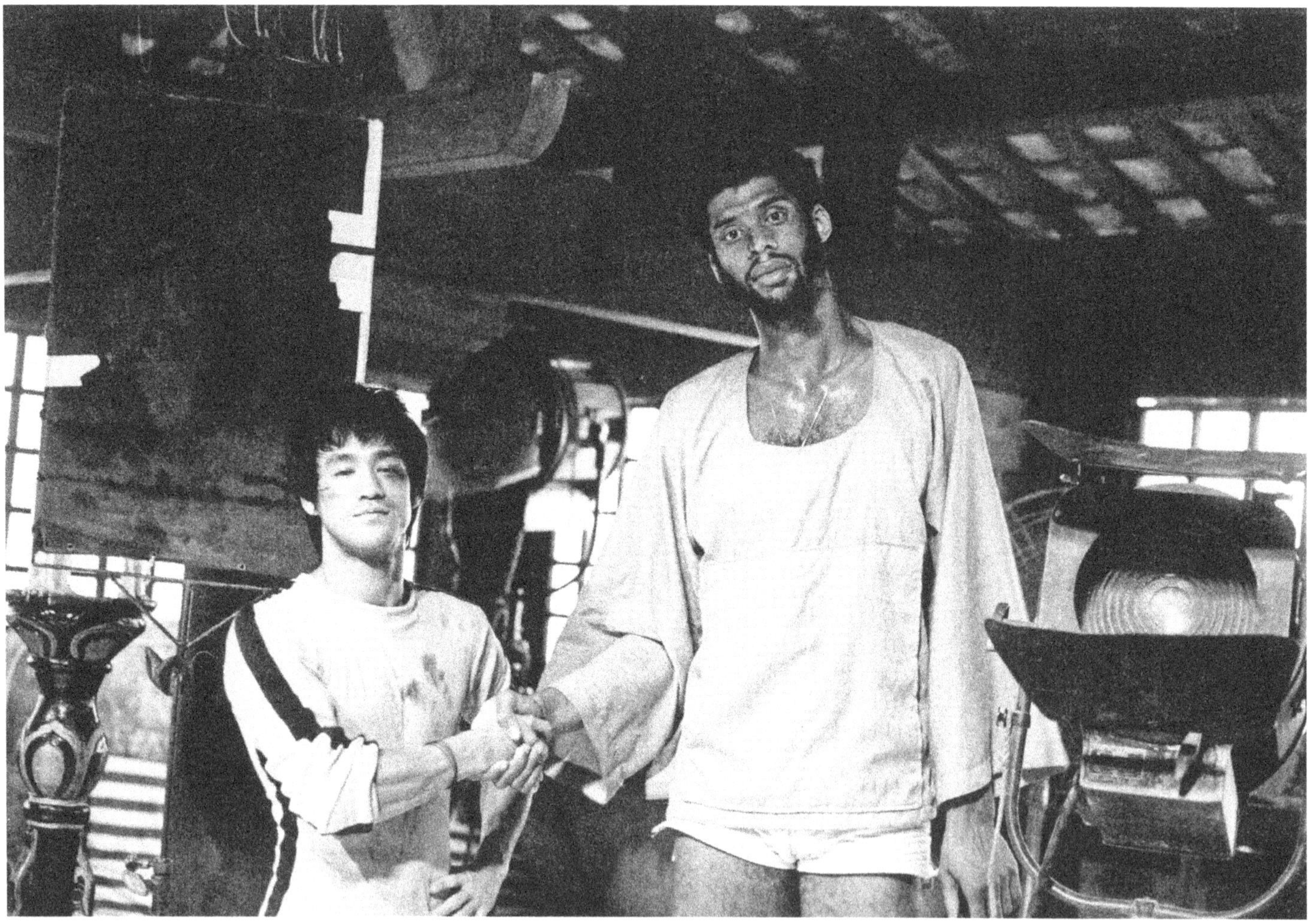

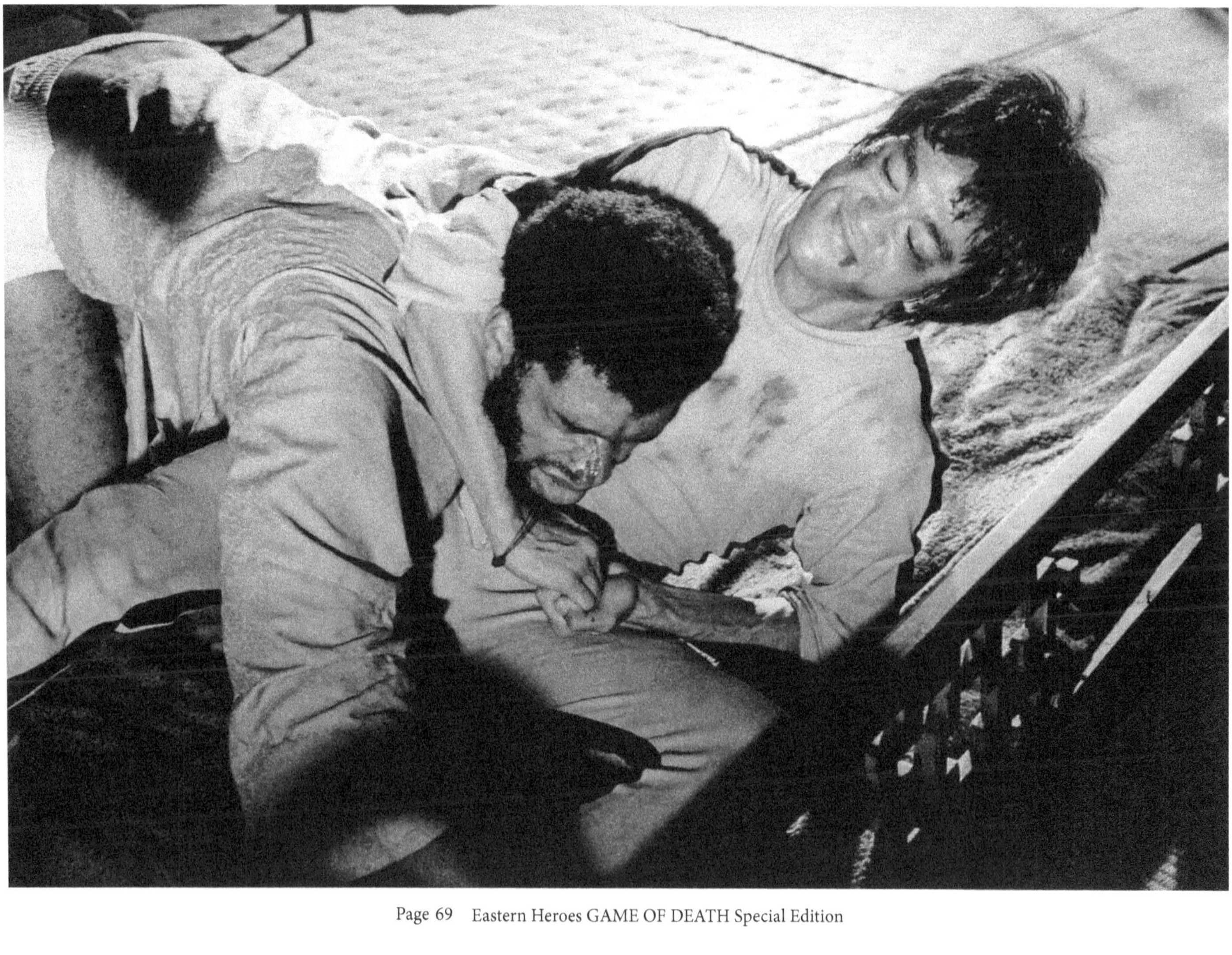

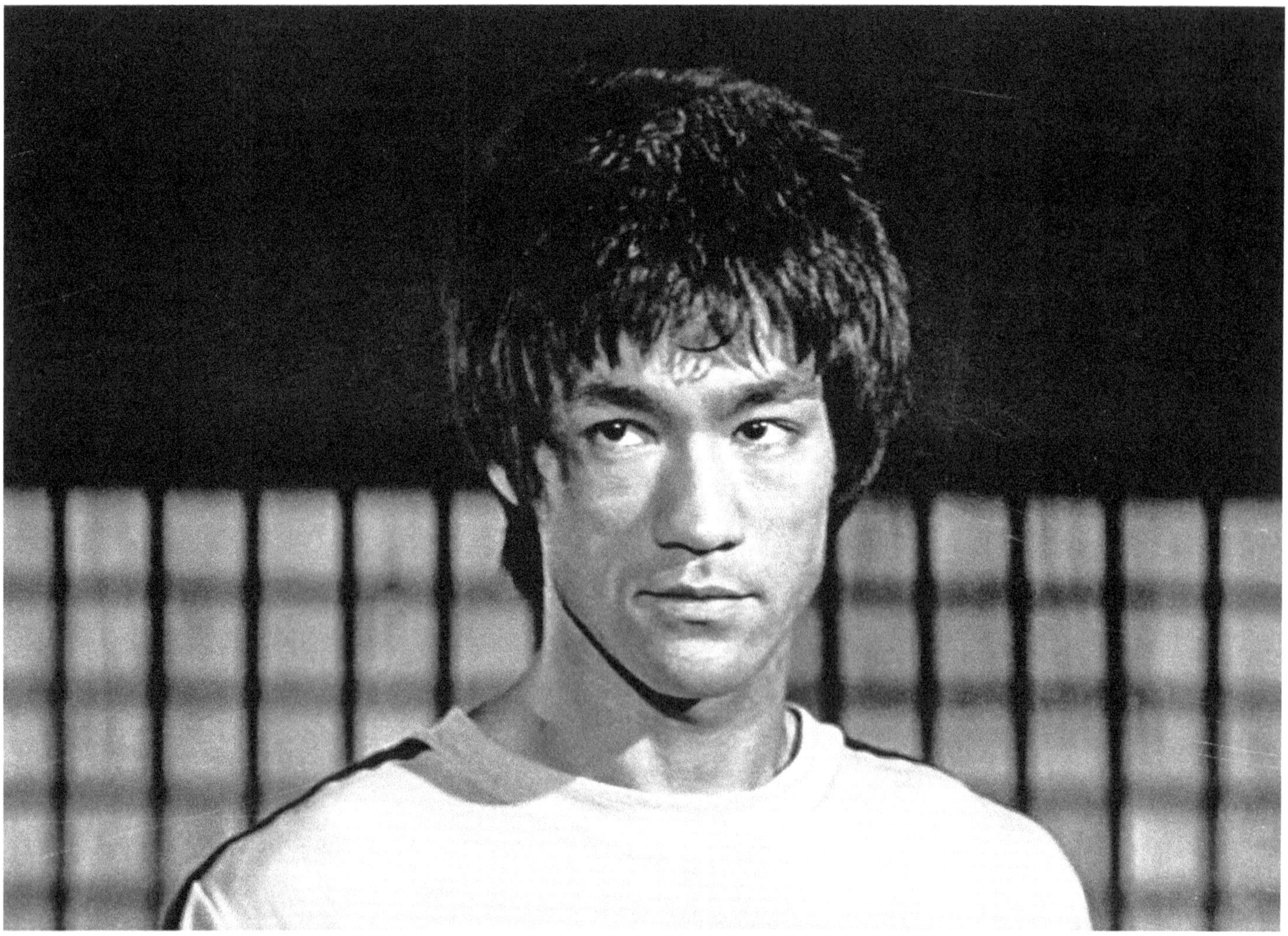

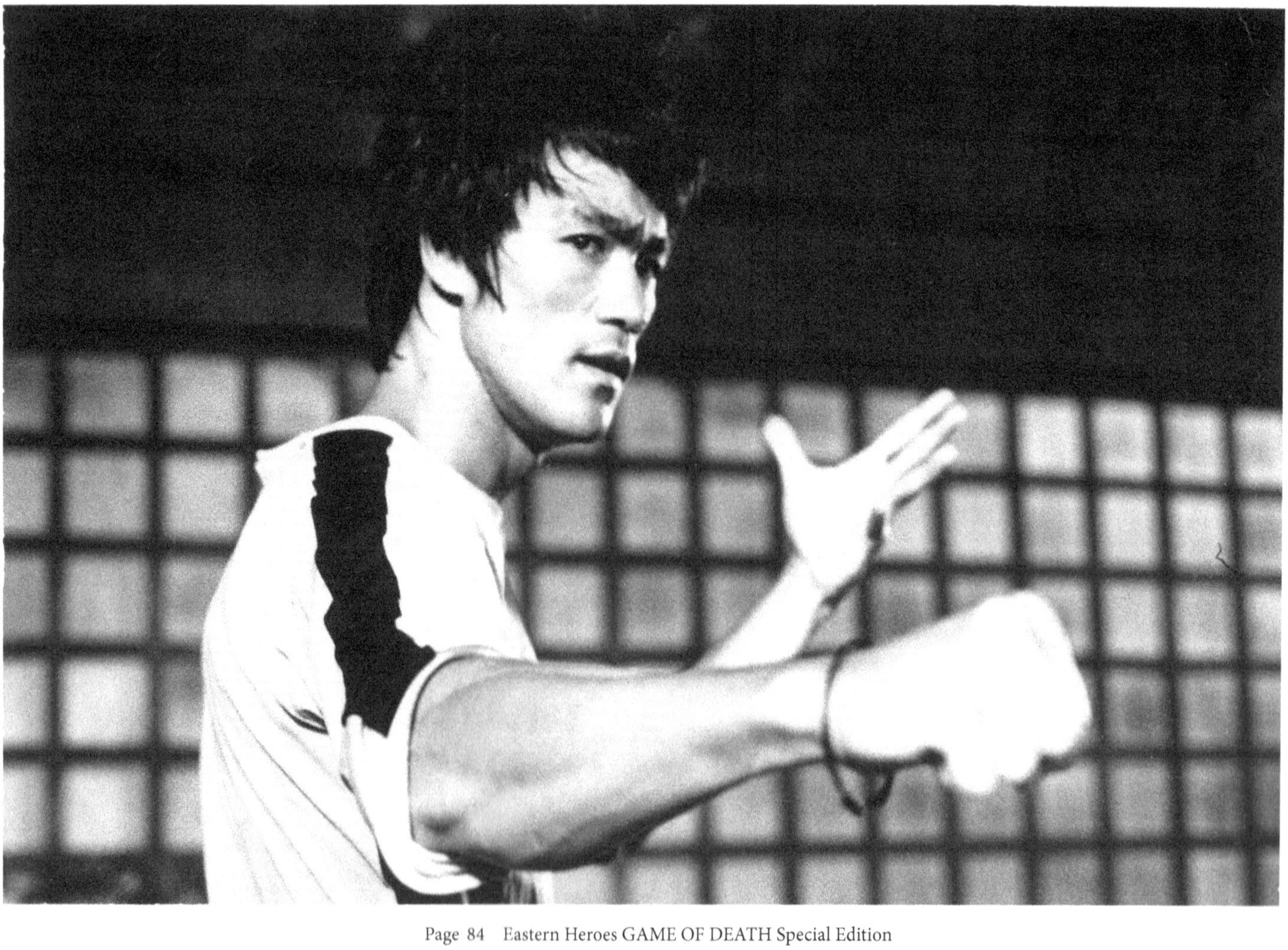

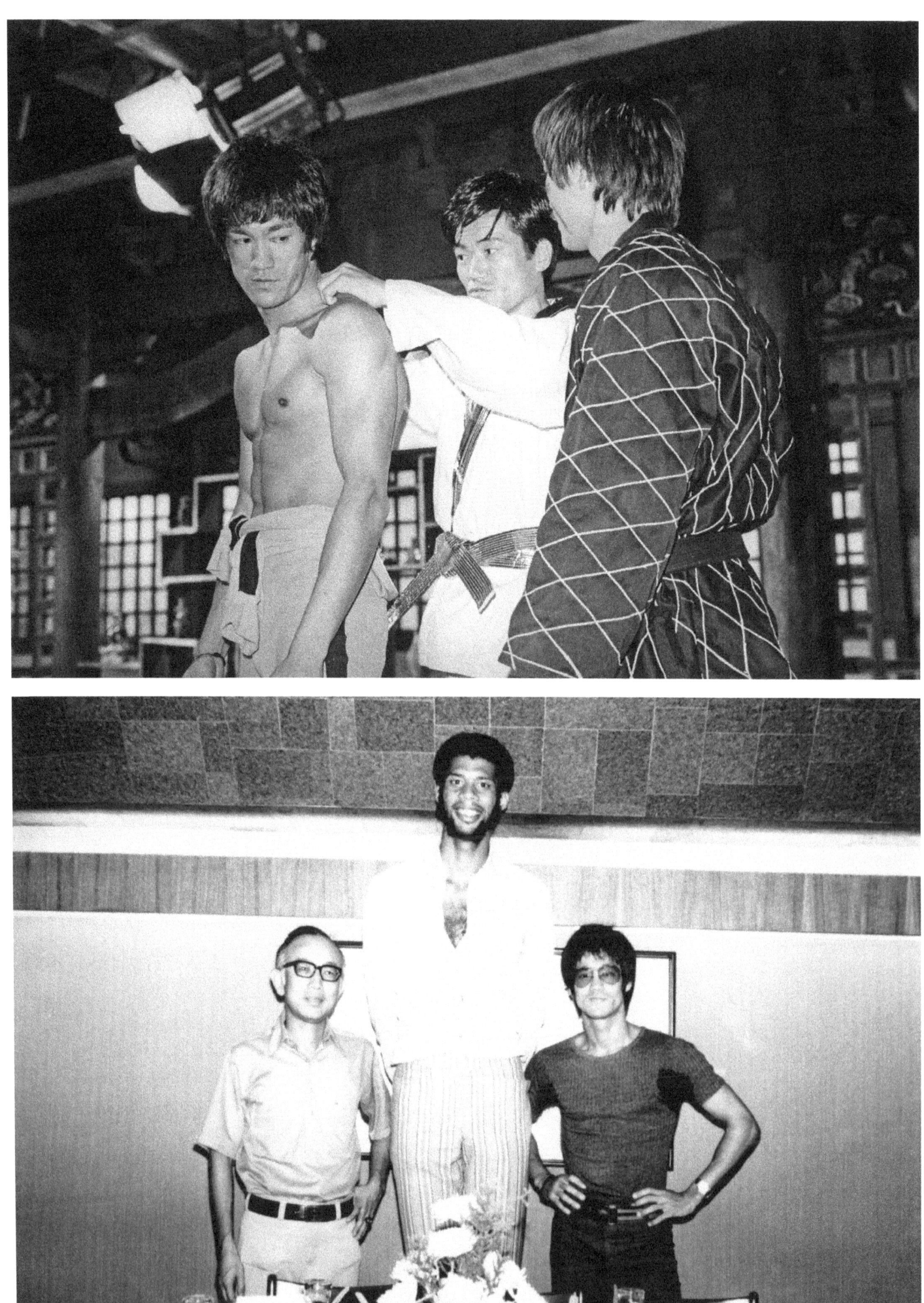

Page 86 Eastern Heroes GAME OF DEATH Special Edition

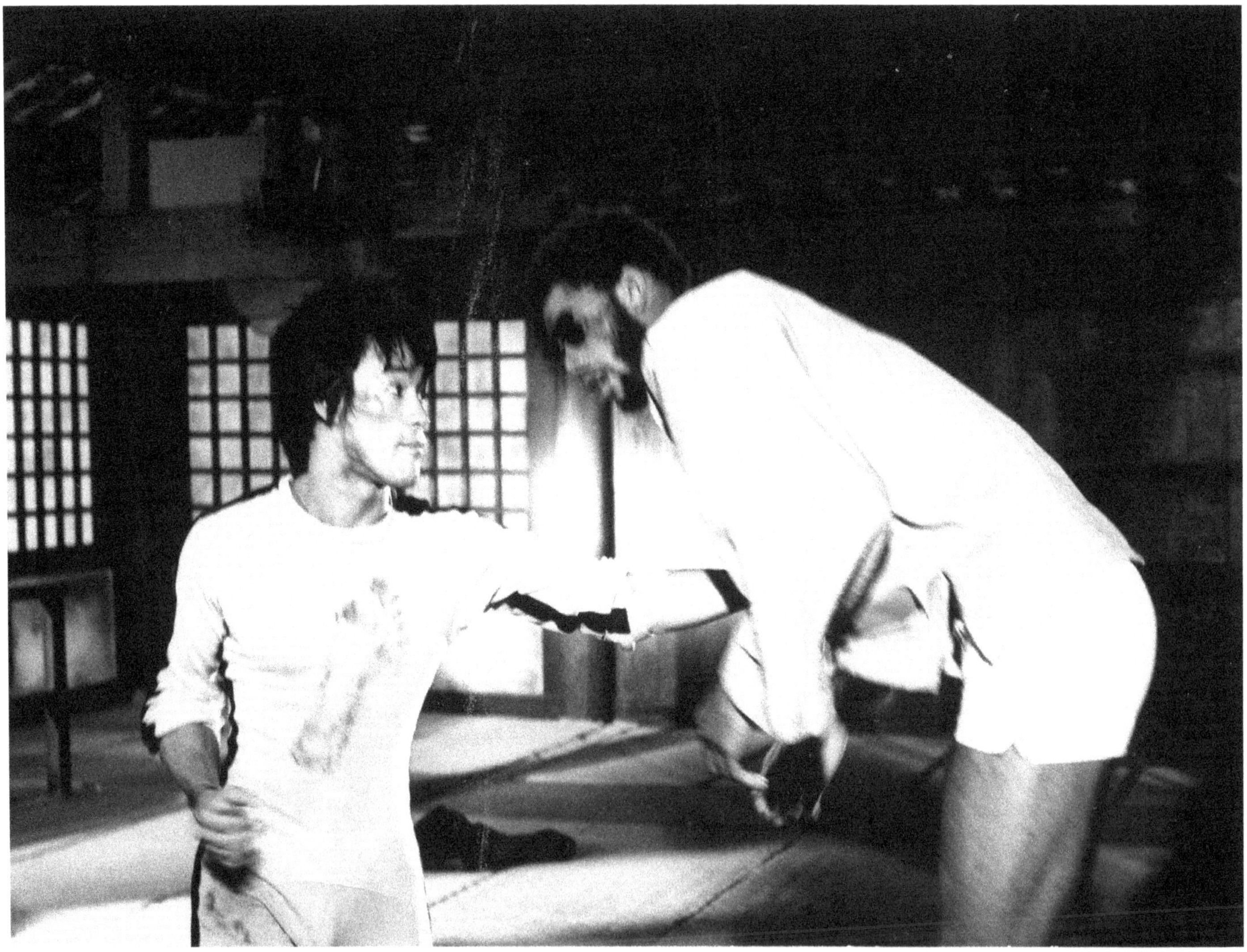

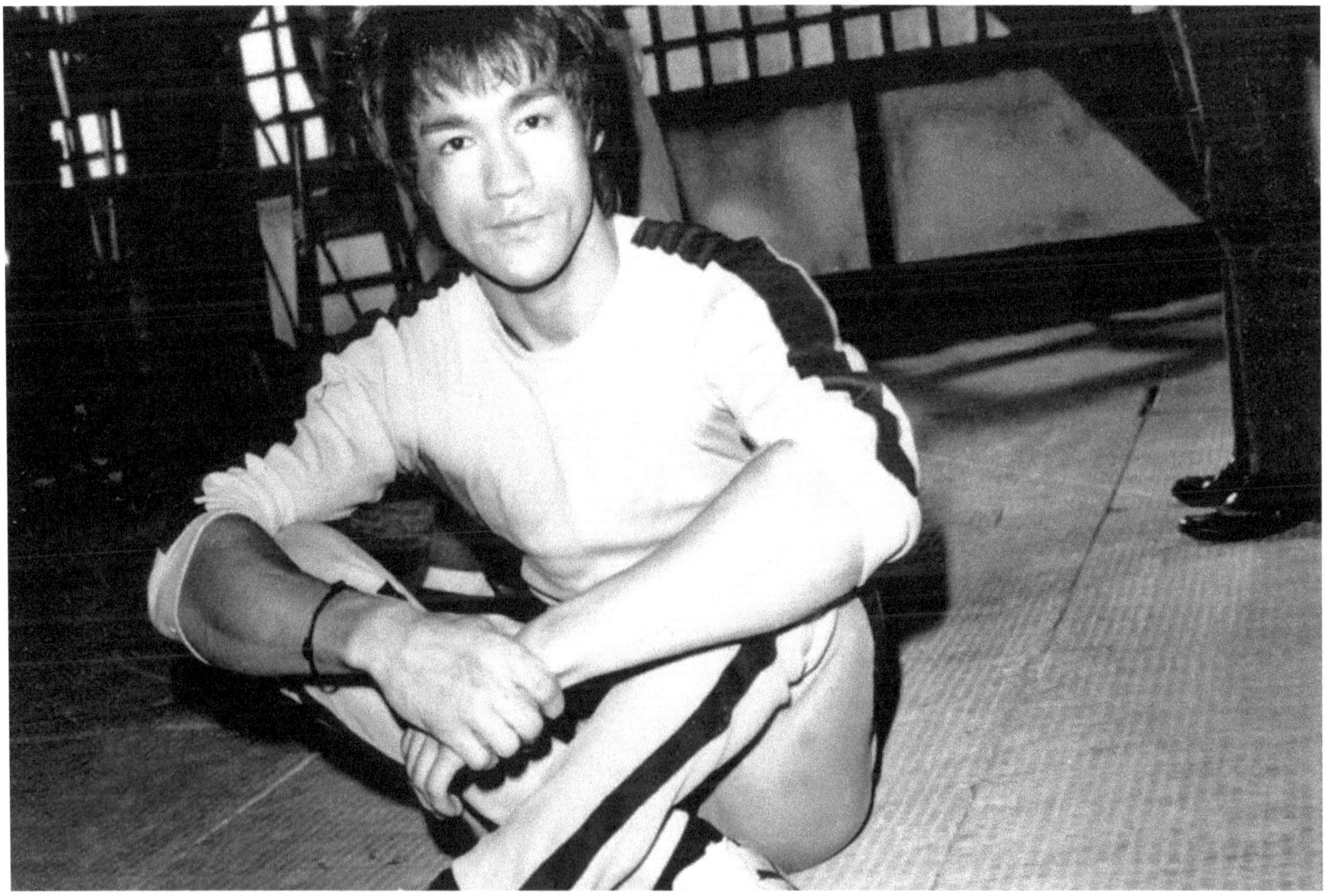

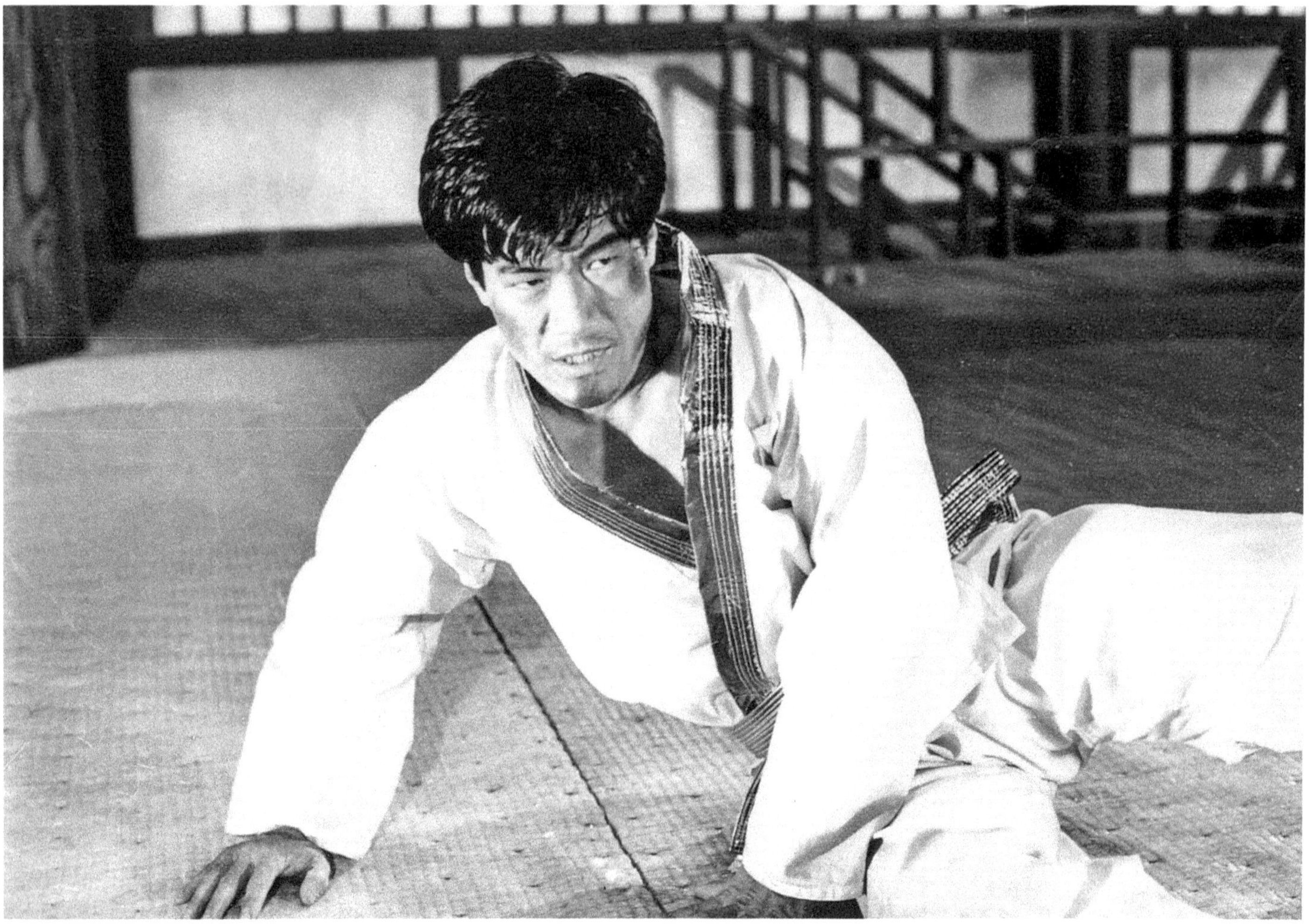

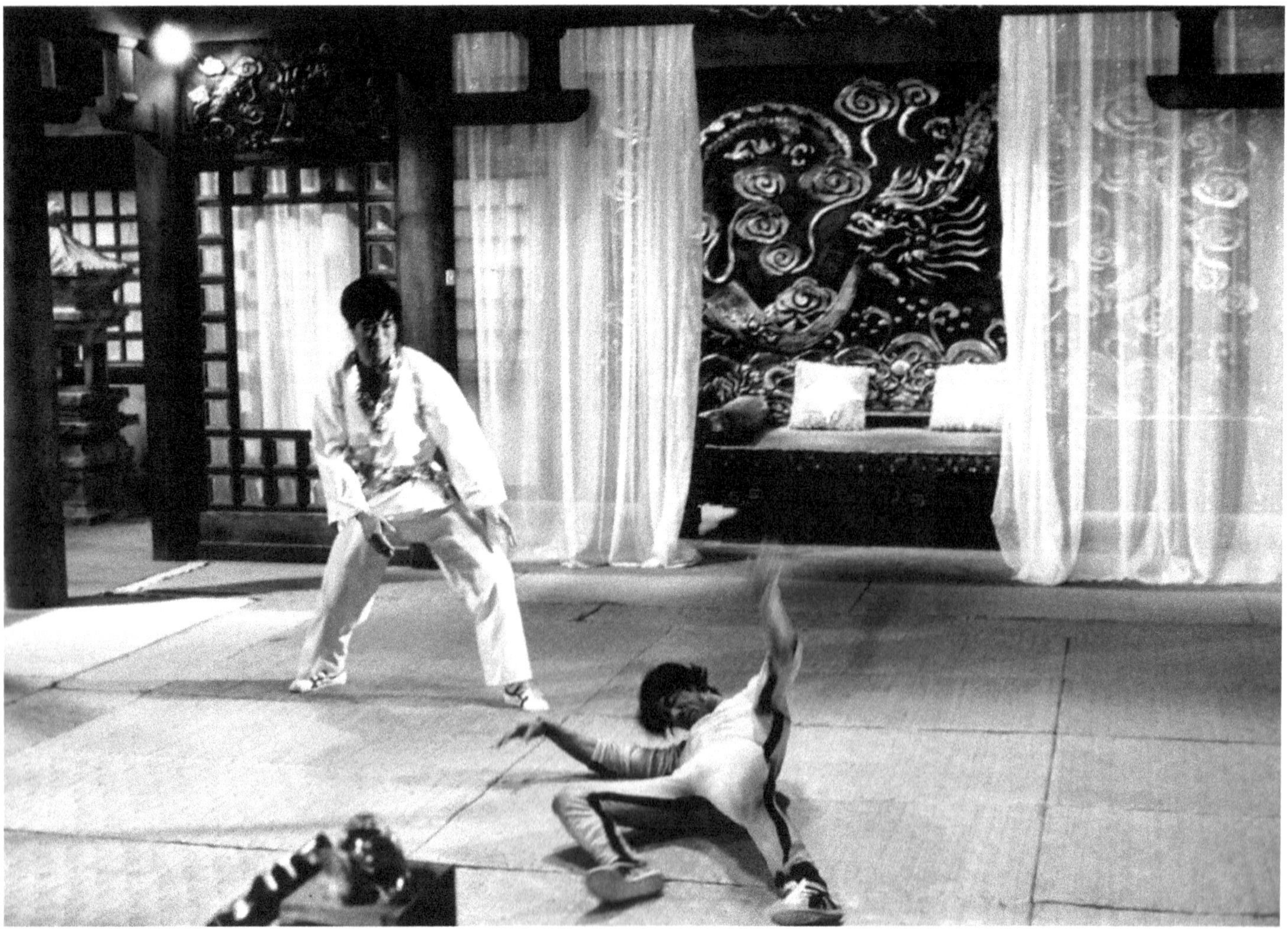

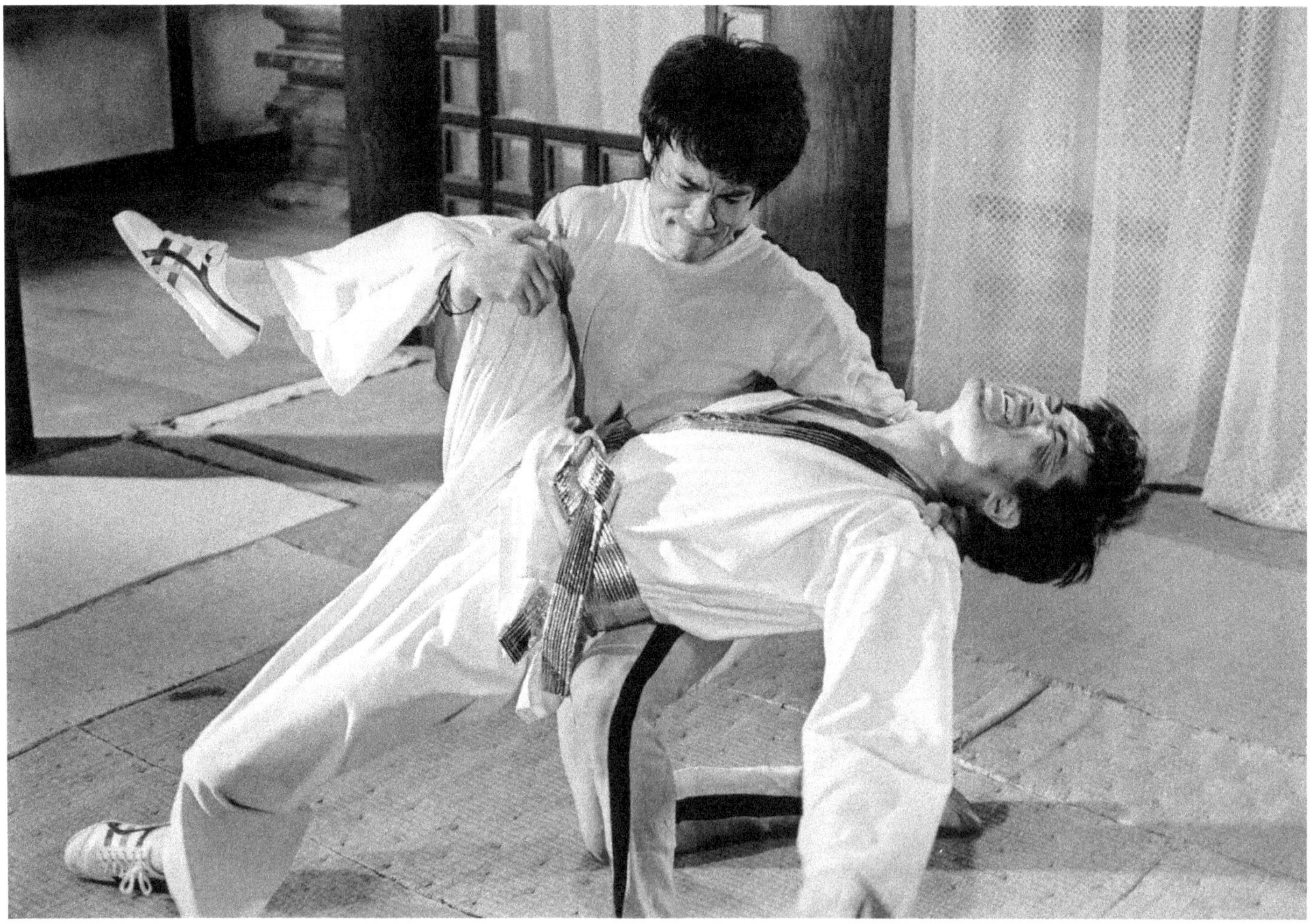

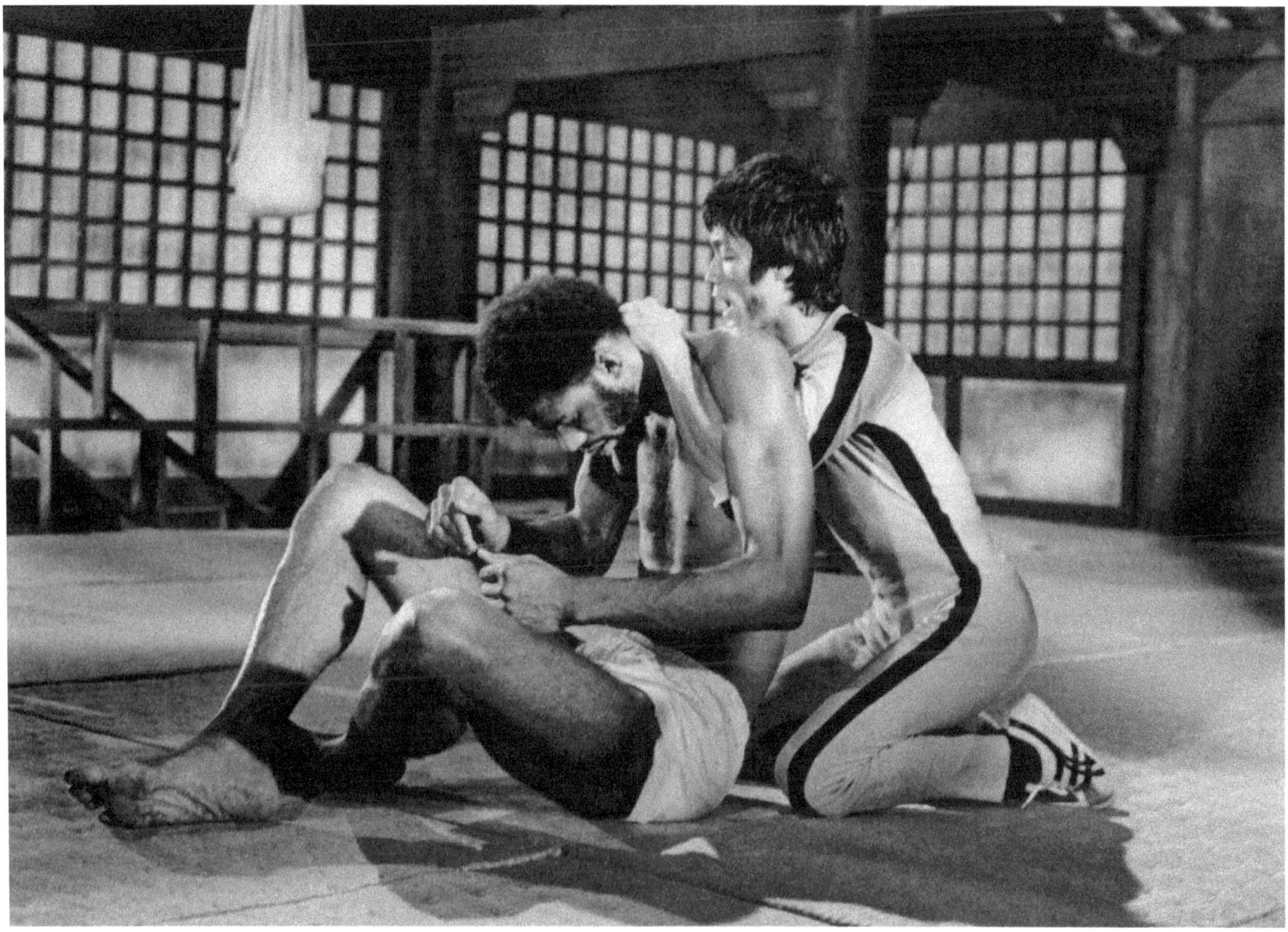

MEMORABILIA

COURTESY OF MICHAEL NESBITT

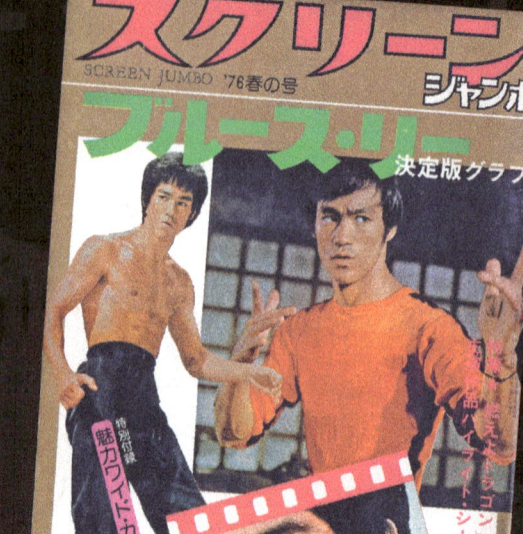

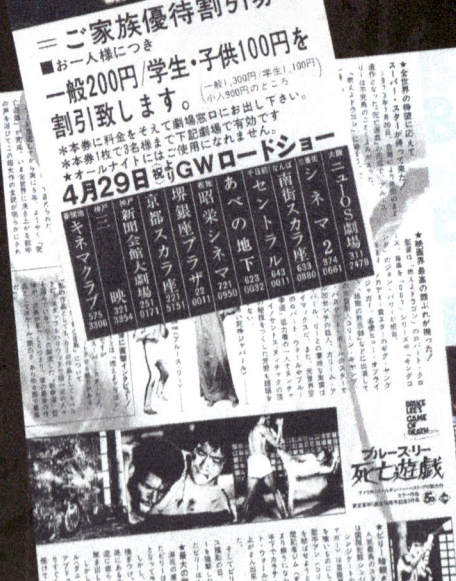

THE POWER OF BRUCE LEE

BOOKS & MAGAZINES

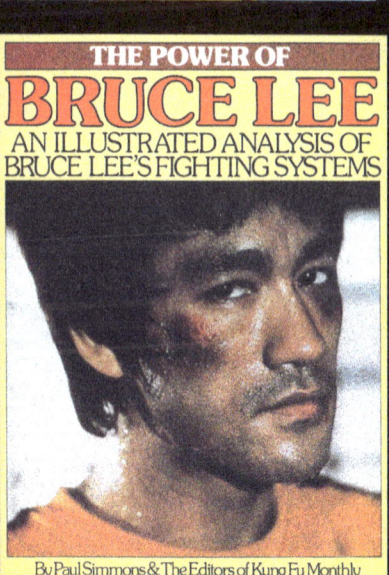

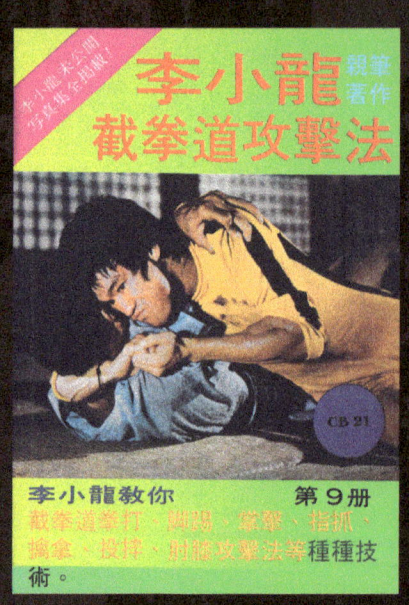

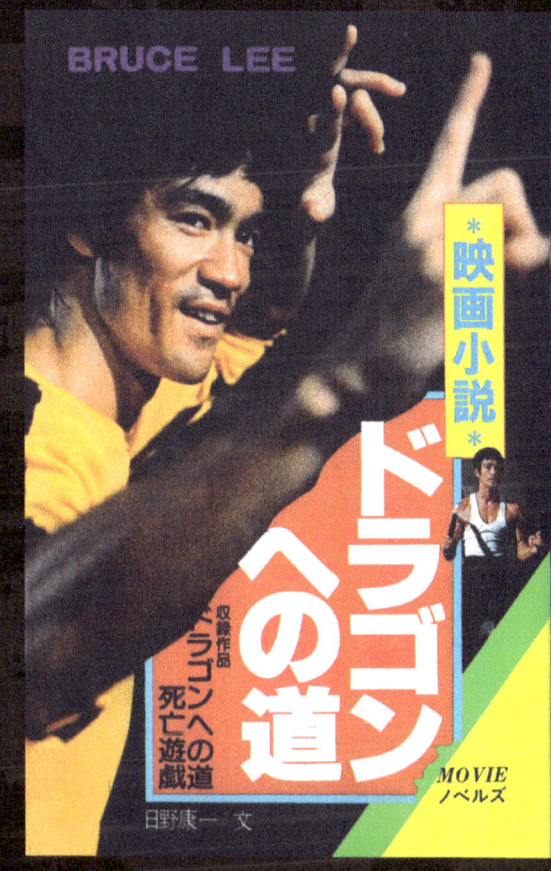

永久完全保存版

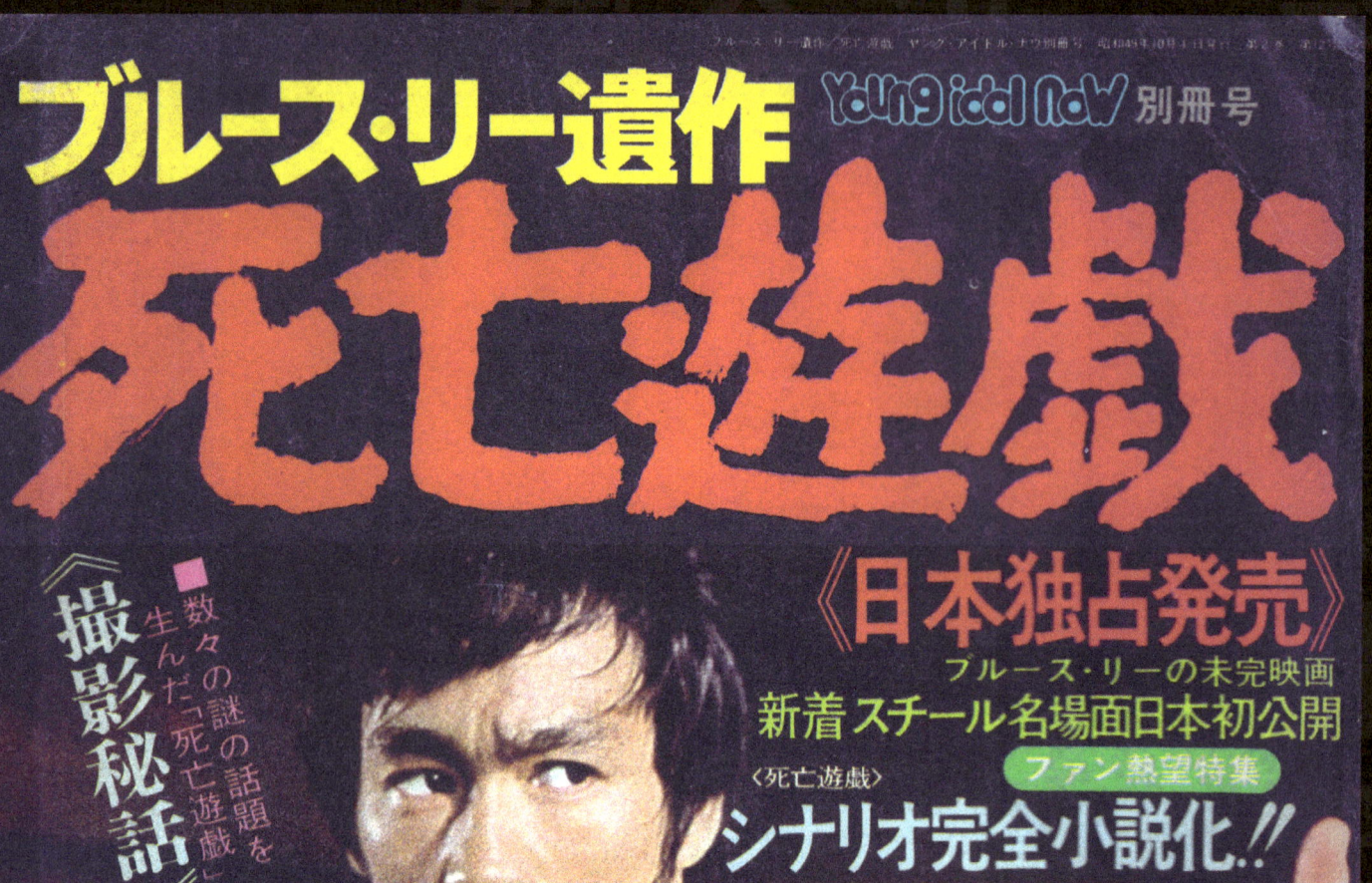

功夫雜誌

KUNG FU

※李小龍秘技——『神道腳』之謎

KC 13

※一流打星對各類武技的見解及心得
※跳繩——最佳的體力與耐力鍛鍊方法
※特殊自衞術　※一招必殺？

港幣三元

KARATE
& oriental arts jan.-feb. no. 76 50p

BRUCE LEE'S GAME OF DEATH

INTERNATIONAL TANG SOO DO

MAY · JUNE 1980
karate
AND ORIENTAL ARTS no 84 60p

"In the Steps of?"

NOV · DEC 1980
karate
AND ORIENTAL ARTS no 87 60p

Gung Lik Kune
Kobudo Weapons
Karate-do

Karate Special

In The Steps Of …

Price £1.50
No. 1

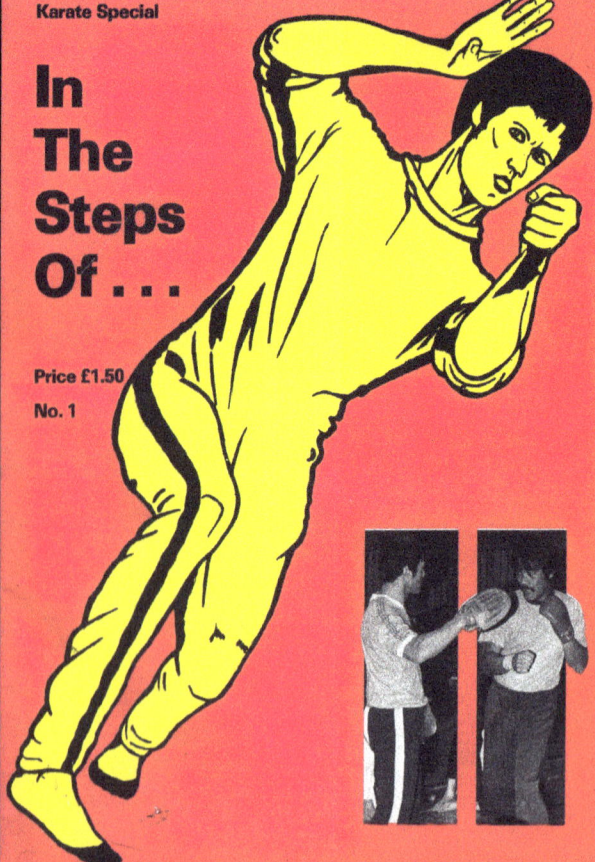

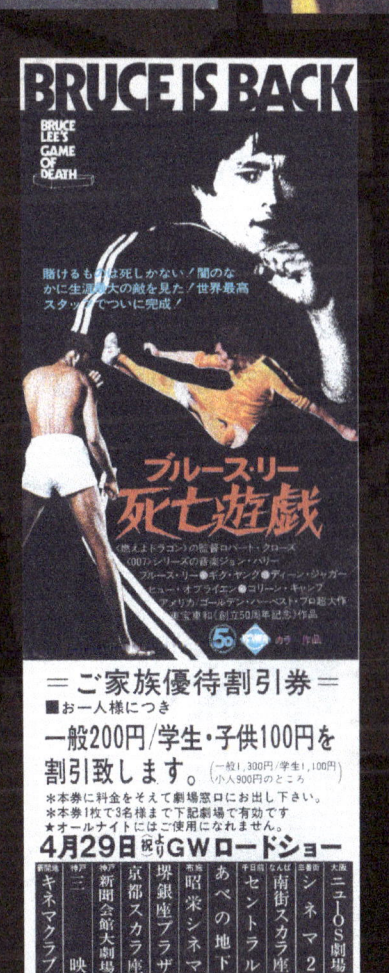

CINEMA TICKETS

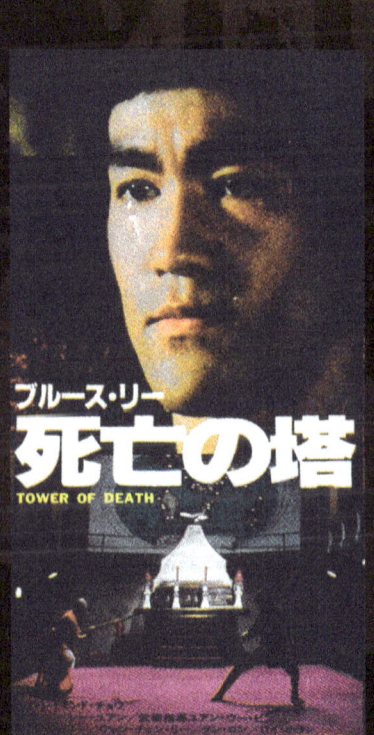

JAPANESE PRESS FLYERS & BOOKS

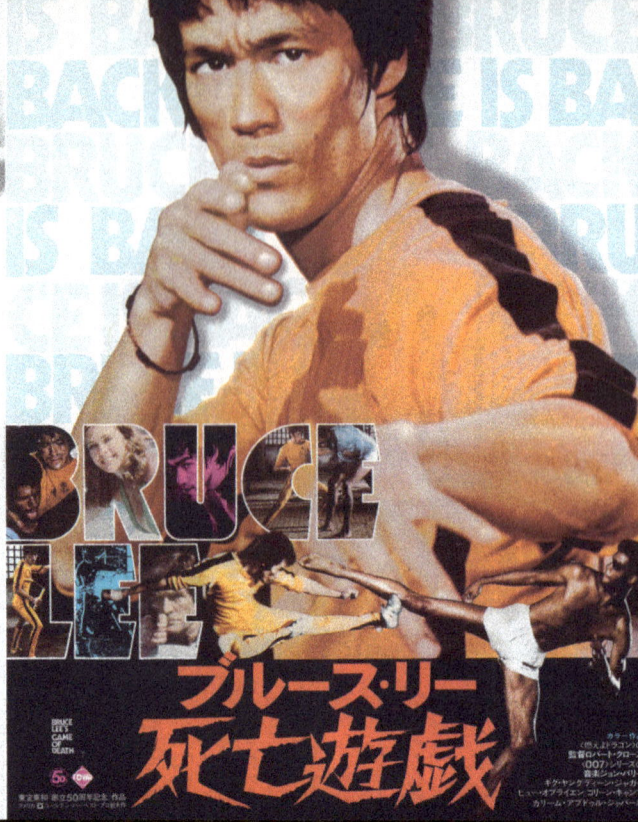

ブルース・リー通信 NO.1

■またやって来る？ドラゴン・ブーム
彗星のように現われ、4本の主演作と未完成の"死亡遊戯"を残し、竜巻きのように消えて早くも4年め、またぞの7月20日――。ひとたびブルース・リー主演の作品として燃えれば、ドラゴン・ブームが甦える。かつてその熱狂振りを知った日本のファンがじっと黙っていたわけはない。NTVで"死亡遊戯"が完成したからと放送された4月6日の夜、噂は全国に広まった。マニアックな熱狂的ファンが、いまだに全国の映画館にたむろして、ブルース・リー映画の上映を待ちわびている。ドラゴン・マニアの情熱には凄まじいものがある。「NTVで"死亡遊戯"を見て、ブルース・リーが再びこの世に蘇えった想いを胸にかきたてている」とファン達は口を揃えて語る。

■世界が待っている！"死亡遊戯"
1972年9月ローマからブルース・リー帰った次回作、"死亡遊戯"、みずからプロデューサー、監督をかって、完成を目前にひかえた1973年7月20日、ブルース・リーは忽然とその姿を消した。フィリピン人・極真拳の名人ダニー・イノサント、韓国合気道の大家、池漢載、バスケットボール界の巨人アブドール・ジャバール、盟友ジェームス・ティエンなど、アクション俳優たちをかり集めて、クライマックスの3階建ての塔の大決戦、約1時間14分のフィルムを完成させていたブルース・リーとドラゴンの絆を心から知悉する人ひとり、ロバート・クローズ監督にハリウッドに引きつぐ。中国武術の達人ジェームス・ユアン、華の奇才クァン・フィッシンなど数多くの関係者の助力を得て、幻の"死亡遊戯"は甦えったのだ。映画は10月公開予定。

■不滅のドラゴン、ブルース・リー小百科
アメリカ中国系である中国人映画スター、武道家、現代史における1人の巨人、李小龍（李は姓、小龍は名、英名はブルース・リー）は、父の地方巡業中の太平洋岸劇団の巡業中サンフランシスコに1940年11月27日に生まれ、幼名「学振藩」（略称「振藩」）を名のり、洗礼名を受けた。生後3か月で両親と香港に戻り、18歳まで香港で育ち、以後はアメリカでの生活となる。以後20年間、彼は幾多の運命に翻弄されながら、ワシントン大学在学中に結婚し、のちに演劇科中退後、アメリカ・ハリウッドで"グリーン・ホーネット"のTV映画で有名になり、1965、1971年、1973年7月20日、中国功夫映画でその名を世界中にとどろかせた。が、その絶頂期にあまりにも早く、その絶頂期にあまりにも夭折した。夫人は白人リンダ（息子ブランドン、娘シャノン）、墓地はシアトル市西北の葬地にある。

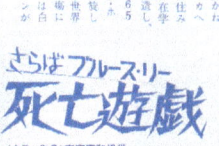 

POSTCARDS

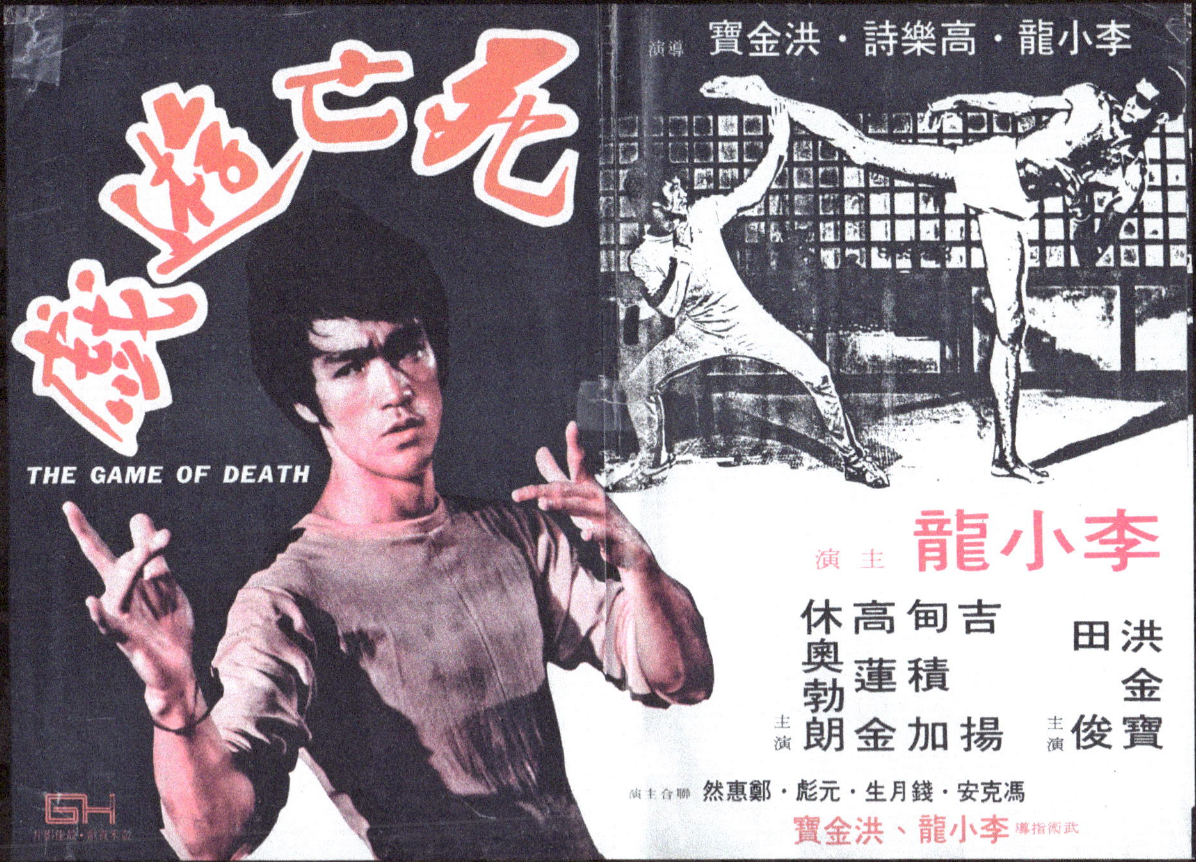
死亡遊戲
THE GAME OF DEATH
李小龍・高樂詩・洪金寶 導演
主演 李小龍
吉揚
甸積加
高蓮金
休奧勃朗 主演
洪金寶
田俊 主演
馮克安・錢月生・元彪・鄭惠然 合主演
武術指導 李小龍、洪金寶

BRUCE LEE'S GAME OF DEATH
BRUCE LEE IN GAME OF DEATH
GIG YOUNG • DEAN JAGGER
COLLEEN CAMP
HUGH O'BRIAN
KAREEM ABDUL-JABBAR "HAKIM"

RENÉ CHATEAU et A.M.L.F. présentent
BRUCE LEE
5 ANS APRÈS SA MORT SON DERNIER COMBAT
LE JEU DE LA MORT
avec
KARIM "ABDULL" JABBAR (2m20 de hauteur)
Mise en scène ROBERT CLOUSE • Produit par RAYMOND CHOW

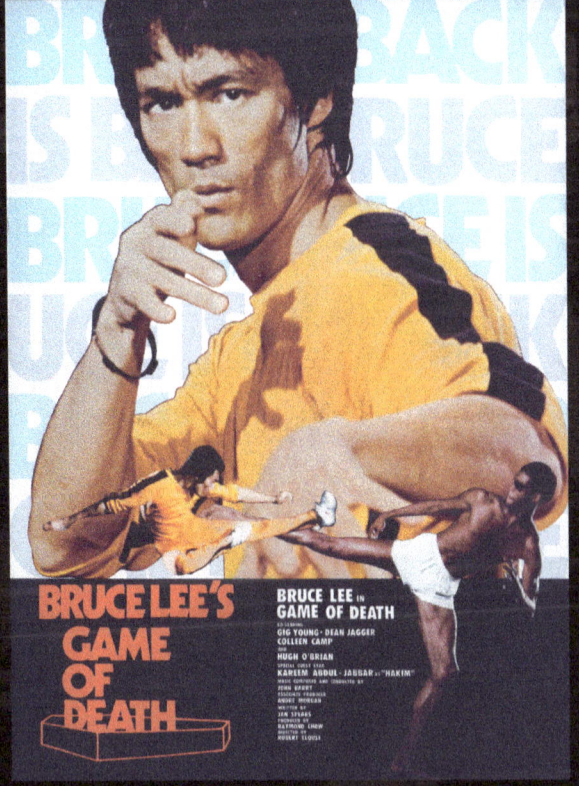

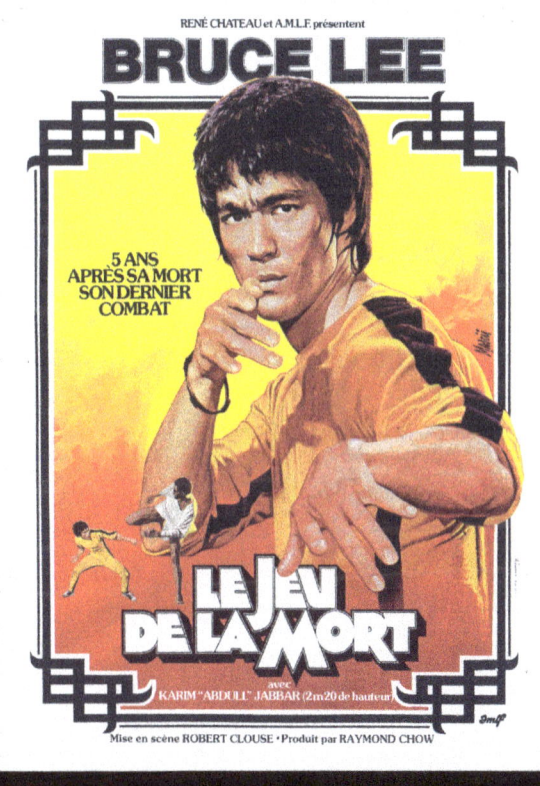

RECORDS - EPs

オリジナル・サウンドトラック盤

シャウト・オブ・リー

RECORDS - LPs

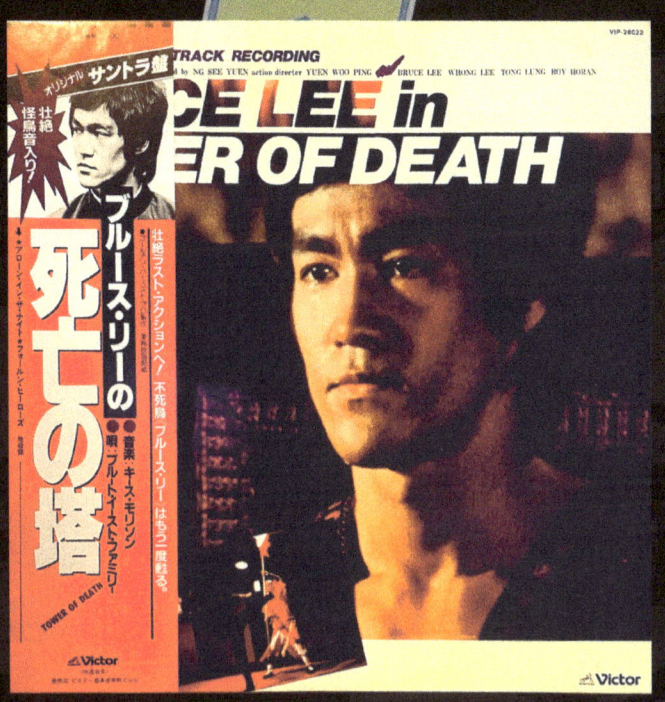

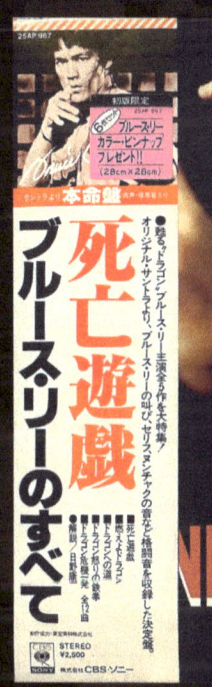

PRESS PACKS

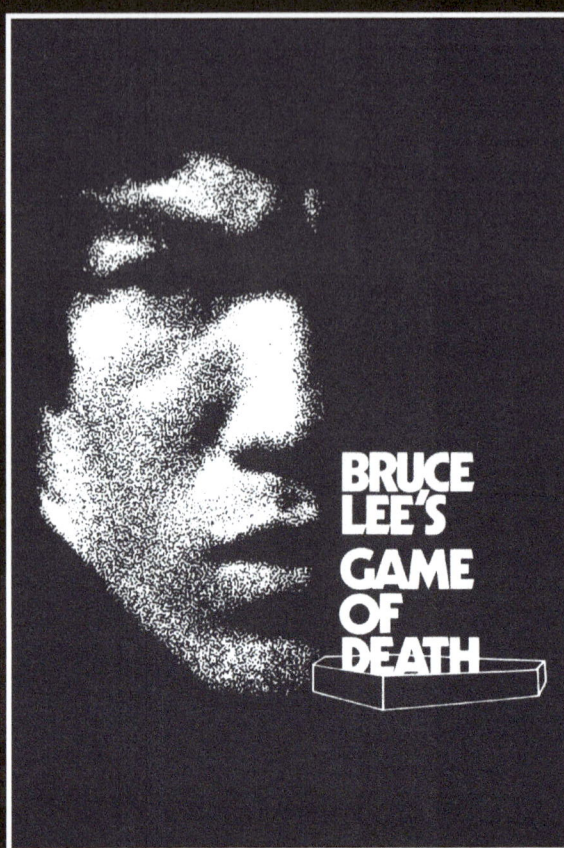

CITY ON FIRE PRESENTS
A CONVERSATION WITH ALAN CANVAN

CONDUCTED BY J.J. BONA

The following is a conversation with indie filmmaker, Alan Canvan. He's a cinema enthusiast and a quote/unquote "Bruce Lee Historian" (more on that later) who has a different – and very controversial – thought process when it comes to his opinions on Bruce Lee and his films, which was one of the reasons I approached him for this interview.

Alan has hosted a few events, including Bamboo, Nunchucks & Dirty Footprints: A Retrospective of Bruce Lee's 'Game of Death', which was co-hosted by Bruce Lee: A Life. author, Matthew Polly; as well as a private screening for Bruce Lee's obscure childhood film, The Orphan (1960), which was made possible thanks to Alan's relentless ability to seek down the film's copyright holders in Hong Kong. He also has written some in-depth articles in the British Bruce Lee publication BLR and Spain's BLM magazine.

But what Alan is perhaps mostly known for The Game of Death Redux, which was released exclusively on Criterion Collection's 2020 boxed set Bruce Lee: His Greatest Hits. The film showcased 23 minutes of the 1972-era Game of Deathfootage that was presented closely the way Bruce intended, while at the same time, keeping in-tact some of the stronger aspects of the universally panned, pieced together 1978 film (known to fans as Game of Death '78), such as John Barry's acclaimed score, as well some of the film's strong audio design.

This brings us to his latest project – an updated, new and improved version of Game of Death Redux (aka Game of Death Redux 2.0), which will soon be released to the public. I thought it would be a good opportunity to have a chat about it, as well as many other topics surrounding Bruce Lee and his work.
Enjoy!

JB: Why did you decide to make 2.0?

AC: What's the adage regarding art never being finished, only abandoned? Yeah. With the initial edit, my focus was entirely on the flow of the piece (i.e., how the shots were cut and how the music drove the narrative.) Artistically, I was satisfied. Technically, there were aspects that bothered me. What I really wanted was a complete visual and sonic restoration. It took over a year to achieve, and I was fortunate enough to work with the right team to arrive at this new version.

JB: For those who have seen the original Redux, what can be expected in version 2.0?

AC: Where do I begin? For starters, the new Redux has been fully restored with a brand-new color grade and audio mix. Additionally, Chris Kent, who looped Bruce's war cries for Robert Clouse's Game of Death movie, lent his voice once again to match the audio portions I used from the 1978 film. He did a stellar job. Finally, I reworked a dozen sequences which resulted in a far more concise and dramatic presentation of the narrative. I can honestly say that Game of Death, in any incarnation, has never looked or sounded better. After three years, I can finally put it to rest.

JB: Fully restored? Does this mean you had access to Game of Death's negatives?

AC: Working with the original negatives would have been ideal, but a film can be restored without scanning the original print. In fact, over the years, quite a few movies have been remastered that way.

JB: We've seen John Little's Warrior's Journey. We've seen Bruce Lee in G.O.D/Art Port. Why should we see Alan Canvan's Game of Death Redux?

AC: The answer lies in what the viewer hopes to gain from the experience. Redux's audience are lovers of cinema as an artform. Many people respond to Bruce Lee as an icon, but don't necessarily see his films as high art - and that's understandable given that most of his movies were hampered by substandard production values and conventions that were far beneath his talent. The Game of Death 1972 footage benefitted from not having to carry the burden and scrutiny of a full-length feature film. However, what truly differentiates it from the rest of Lee's cinematic oeuvre is the level of artistry that he brought to the picture: his shot compositions, costume/set designs and fight choreography were truly avant-garde, but that often gets overlooked in favor of the spectacle. My goal is to dispel the broad clichés associated with Bruce Lee and give weight to his cinematic brilliance. Game of Death Redux is really an arthouse film disguised as a Kung Fu flick. In that respect, its worthy of being discussed alongside the cinema of Kubrick and Kurosawa.

"My goal is to dispel the broad clichés associated with Bruce Lee and give weight to his cinematic brilliance."

JB: So, you're saying that Redux is more for those Bruce Lee fans who own an Akira Kurosawa collection; than the ones who own the Fast & Furious collection?

AC: The question pigeonholes the viewer. At the end of the day, it's entirely possible for someone to love Fast & Furious, yet also be moved by Redux.

JB: The Trailer for Game of Death Redux. Can you explain the voice over?

AC: Some assumed that it was a trailer narrator, but it's really the American mercenary who befriends Bruce's character prior to the mission. This role was going to be played by Bob Baker. The V.O. is Kincaid speaking to Hai Tien the night before they leave for the temple. You're the first to ask me about this, Jeff, so kudos for giving me the opportunity to clarify.

JB: No problem. Is it exclusive to the Trailer, or will it also make an appearance in Game of Death Redux?

AC: I wrote it exclusively for the trailer.

JB: You brought back Chris Kent (who dubbed Bruce's war cries for the 1978 movie) for the Game of Death Redux. Why him? Why not use Bruce's existing battle cries and/or recreate his sound?

AC: This was a huge sticking point for me with the first iteration of Redux. In retrospect, I feel it was too much of a compromise to go with the hybrid of Bruce and Chris's voices. The main issue with attempting to apply Lee's existing war cries from other films to Game of Death is that, tonally, the audio doesn't match up with his lip movements in the footage. Moreover, audiences are so familiar with those battle cries that, subliminally, it detracts from Game of Death's identity and comes off as the sonic cut 'n' paste job that it is. Many don't consider the experimental nature of Bruce's war cries and believe them to have been identical in each of his movies. They weren't, as he was still in the early stages of developing this personal cinematic vocabulary that was so unique to him. Nowhere is this more evident than in Game of Death, where, often, his expressions are deliberately over the top. Chris's dubbing for the '78 film syncs beautifully with the material, and that, to me, superseded attempting to force a square peg into a round hole. And yes, I realize there's irony in my citing Lee's unique trademark, only to have another

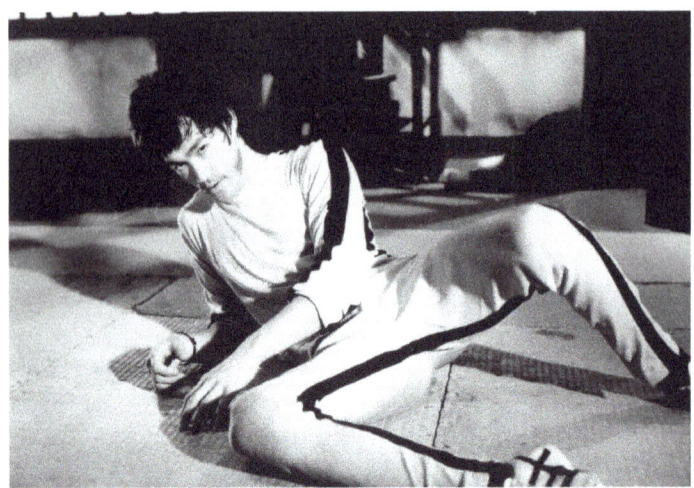
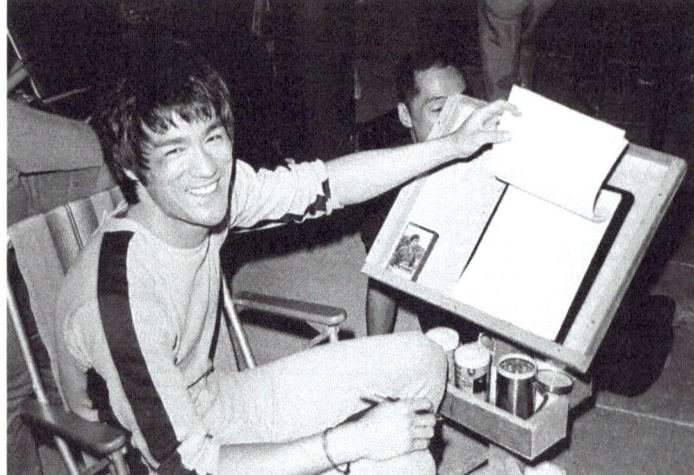

individual voice him. But the spirit of Lee's work is there, and Chris's audio for the remaining footage gave the battle cries a consistency that was missing in the previous edit. You're a huge fan of the 1978 film, so what's your take?

JB: Yes. A huge fan of Game of Death '78. After The Big Boss, it's my favorite Bruce Lee film, given the fact that I've watched it more than almost any existing film I can think of. It fires on all cylinders. Even the rusty ones. For that – and the then-mystery of its flattened '72 GOD footage – it's interesting, entertaining and gives me an experience that even a "real" Bruce Lee film can't compete with. The reason I ask why you brought back Chris Kent is because I'm a fan of every second of "audio" coming from Game of Death '78, which includes Kent's battle cries. There's something "clean as a whistle" about them, especially when compared to Bruce Lee's own screechy battle cries. And like you said, why take his cries from Enter the Dragon or something and force-fit them in? Totally understandable. The funny thing is when most people do their Bruce Lee impersonation, the sound that comes out of peoples' mouth sounds more like the cries Kent laid down on Game of Death '78, than those of Bruce's real cries from Enter the Dragon.

AC: Agreed, nearly all the war cry impersonators rely on Chris's voice for reference. I think a big part of the '78 film's appeal is that it really plays like a heightened biopic of the last year and a half of Bruce's life. But it's the subtle way in which Clouse draws those parallels that impress me. Tiny details, like Billy's wardrobe choices and photographs of Lee's childhood films adorning his dressing room, to name a few.

JB: Makes one wonder if organized crime syndicates – wanting a piece of Bruce's career – was another parallel Clouse might have worked into the "heightened biopic." Thoughts?

AC: It's no secret that the entertainment world, on occasion, has had ties to organized crime. Do I believe Lee was being pressed by Triads? Not directly. There are a couple of reasons I say this: First, his rise to superstardom in Hong Kong happened within the span of a year, so we're talking about a very narrow window of time. Second, Bruce was an American expat living in Hong Kong, and, because of this, it would've been significantly more difficult to exert control over his career than it would have with another local celebrity.

"Bruce Lee wanted and needed the world to perceive him as the baddest man on the planet (pre-Mike Tyson!) Through the magic of cinema, he got his wish"

JB: During the peak of his stardom, it was said that Bruce carried a gun, right?
AC: Yeah. And that's pretty revealing, isn't it? Who or what did he have to fear? The answer is both simple and complex. A topic that's rarely, if ever, discussed is the immense psychological effect that fame had on Lee. I'm not referring to the usual pressures of celebrity. Bruce Lee wanted and needed the world to perceive him as the baddest man on the planet (pre-Mike Tyson!) Through the magic of cinema, he got his wish. It put him in a precarious position though, as a great deal of his mental energy became focused on maintaining this illusion to the public. He wasn't really concerned whether someone could defeat him (Lee felt he was indestructible) as he was alert to the fact that someone could possibly get the drop on him and shatter the myth that he was untouchable. What are the psychological repercussions of attempting to maintain that standard? A heavy toll. Between this and the beginnings of a major drug habit, his paranoia would have been at its zenith. It's understandable why he felt the need to carry a gun. His is a classic cautionary tale of 'be careful what you wish for.'

JB: Beginnings of a major drug habit. A gun close by always. Sounds a little like Elvis Presley, especially during his last few years.

AC: There are parallels for sure, even in the near religious zeal of their respective fan bases. But remember, by that time, there was already a widespread wariness in the wake of the Manson murders. In a way, this senseless, horrific act came to symbolize a loss of innocence for America, and many struggled with an existential anxiety in the years that followed. Bruce and Elvis were amongst those affected.

JB: For Game of Death Redux, what kind of character development/backstory did you have for Hai Tien?

AC: I've often said that, of all of Lee's screen characters, Hai Tien comes the closest to Bruce's real-life persona. I did write a comprehensive backstory for the character to clarify who he was independent of Bruce Lee. During this process, I discovered that, while Hai Tien is Lee's alter-ego, there are distinct differences between them.

JB: How comprehensive did you get? Novel material?

AC: Not novel, but pretty granular. I did this for all the main characters.

JB: Wow. Can you share more on Hai Tien's background?

AC: Absolutely. I concluded that Hai Tien was born in Los Angeles to an American mother and Chinese father. He's the only child to an upper middle-class family that wavered between living in Los Angeles and Hong Kong for a decade, before eventually settling in San Diego around the time Hai Tien began middle school. The experience of growing up in two different cultures has influenced his worldview, just as his rebellious nature has shaped his identity.

JB: That's interesting. He's supposed to be a retired martial arts champ, right?

AC: Indeed. He became fascinated with the martial arts at the age of seven but didn't begin his formal training until he was fourteen years old. At the age of twenty-four he became the lightweight martial arts champion of the world and spent the following six years competing against and defeating the highest ranked fighters in the sport. His level of fame would be comparable to Sugar Ray Leonard's in the early 1980's.

JB: The idea that he was "forced to fight" never truly came across on any of the previous versions of the '72 footage (and it was definitely disjointed from the '78 narrative as a whole). He looks as though he's having fun, with no real regard for anyone's safety on (and in some ways, even off) screen. The smiles. The taunts. The humor. Doesn't seem like there's anything on the line for him.

AC: Yes, for me, it was revelatory to look at those characteristics in relation to his circumstances. Similar to Bruce's original outline, my treatment begins with him recently retired and travelling with his wife and young son (not his sister and younger brother) from Los Angeles to Japan. During a layover in Hong Kong's Kai-Tak airport, he's interviewed by the local press, where I emphasize that, although his outward expression and attitude are distinctly American, the people of Hong Kong claim him as their national hero and prodigal son. At the terminal, he's questioned by a reporter on his reasons for retiring, to which he responds: "Fighting stopped being a challenge. To tell the truth, I can beat anyone in the world." The second sentence, which was said by Bruce Lee in a magazine interview, intentionally blurs the line, but more importantly, gives acumen to Hai Tien's character and provides a basis for his metaphysical journey throughout the story. The cockiness he exhibits, in part, is an extension of the psychological armor he has built over a ten-year period of being in the public eye. It's not a performance per se, rather, a true confidence that's rooted in competence. What interested me was exploring these facets of his personality in relation to the concept of ego-death, and its subsequent spiritual rebirth, which to me, is the central theme and emotional nucleus of the film. It's the same story that Lee wrote, only told through the lens of a character study. These elements may or may not have been as relevant to Lee, but they inform me as a storyteller.

JB: Spiritual rebirth? Hold on, what about all that stuff John Little wrote about, such as the Korean underworld gangs and Hai Tien's family being kidnapped?

AC: What about it? That was just the set up to get him to the pagoda, and the aspect of the story that least interested Bruce. His true passion was the story inside the pagoda, and he used the structure itself to represent Hai Tien's unconscious mind. Each hall explores a different layer of his psyche and transforms the setting into a chamber piece with the players never leaving the location and the narrative relying entirely on the performance. I open Redux with a shot of the pagoda in shadow, and sunlight gradually illuminating the temple. This was a deliberate choice. To me, it's comparable to a stage curtain being drawn back and revealing the setting of a play. It also parallels a moment in the film when Kareem's character, who symbolically personifies Hai Tien's dark side, projects the huge Nosferatu like shadow on the wall while removing his gown.

JB: I notice that Bruce and Ji wear similar Asics style sneakers. Is this significant?

AC: I believe it is. Bruce wears two distinct brands of yellow sneakers, neither of which are Asics. Initially, they appear to be, but upon closer inspection they are revealed to be an unknown label that resemble the Panther/Moon Star brands. To me, the sneaker correlation further connects Ji's character, who assumes the role of the Dragon, to Bruce Lee, whom the Dragon is commonly associated with.

JB: And how about the significance of the gold trim on Ji Han-Jae's uniform, not to mention him lying in bed, as if he's waiting for a lover?

AC: Lee deliberately had Ji's character resting in a reclining Buddha position with his hand and arm supporting his head. In Buddhism, this pose represents the final stage of earthly life before attaining nirvana. This subliminally puts forth the idea that, with each ascending battle, Hai Tien is approaching a spiritual awakening. His emotional truth drives the narrative, but it's through the physical trials that he attains enlightenment. Bruce specifically designed the gold trim and belt to equate Ji's character with ancient Emperors, who often claimed the symbol of the Dragon to signify their regality and fierceness.

JB: Even the most diehard of Bruce Lee fans wouldn't focus on these details and their meanings. To most, it's another action film, and other than the whole "be adaptable" message, most of this stuff will go over the casual fans head. So, this is the Kubrick part of Game of Death you must be talking about? Also, if we look hard enough, can't we pull out some Kubrick-like symbolism from any Bruce Lee movie? (Or any movie for that matter)?

AC: I'm certain there are others who fixate on this stuff, but, as you noted, for the majority, the running JKD tutorial in the Hall of the Tiger takes center stage. Few see beyond it and continue to wonder who or what Kareem's character is meant to be. When Lee spoke of making "multi-level films," the level of depth in his intent was lost in translation. I stress that in early 1972 Bruce was truly in the process of forming his own personal brand of martial art films. In an interview with Black Belt Magazine, he described The Silent Flute project as "the Easy Rider of martial art films." This gives tremendous insight into his aesthetic and vision. Could one identify symbolism in Lee's previous films? Sure. The Coliseum battle with Chuck Norris in Way of the Dragon comes to mind – but only the fight itself, not the movie. I wrote an essay for the latest issue of BLR that addresses the principal themes in The Big Boss, which, from an acting and narrative perspective, is his best film. Neither, however, come close to the subject matter in Game of Death. Going back to your question regarding symbolism being recognizable in any movie, I'll answer that with a twist on the old standard – it's not the tale, but he/she who tells it. That's what differentiates a great storyteller from a mediocre one.

JB: What do you think prompted him to go in the more psychological/spiritual direction, as opposed to say another Kung Fu comedy like Way of the Dragon?

AC: Way of the Dragon was the perfect vehicle for Bruce to discover his strengths and weaknesses as a filmmaker. It allowed

him to test the waters without having to contend with the critical reception of a worldwide release. As a film, many of the action scenes work well, but the execution of the larger story falls flat. However, it was innovative in that it created the martial art/comedy sub-genre that Jackie Chan would later go on to perfect. Following his directorial debut, Lee had more confidence as a director to begin revisiting the material he had spent three years developing for The Silent Flute. His initial offering, a script treatment dubbed Southern Fist, Northern Leg, shared DNA with the aborted project: a martial artist faces various physical and psychological trials in his quest to obtain a sacred book that he believes will give him martial enlightenment. Southern Fist, Northern Leg deviates from its predecessor by changing the setting to a Chinese period piece and using the young man's physical and spiritual training to mythologize the origin of Jeet Kune Do. Game of Death's pagoda sequence took it a step further by incorporating the Jungian symbolism in Silliphant's Silent Flute screenplay. Both projects reflect the type of martial art movies he aimed for.

"Way of the Dragon was innovative in that it created the martial art/comedy sub-genre that Jackie Chan would later go on to perfect"

JB: You didn't mention Fist of Fury?
AC: There's a reason it's my least favorite of his movies. In terms of narrative, the beginning of the film is far superior to the slow-moving and fragmented finale. Apart from a few scenes, I find Lee's Chambara driven performance to be too presentational, and fairly one note. In many ways, it's the antithesis of the wonderful representational offering he gave in The Big Boss. Having said that, I do love the first battle in the dojo as well as Bruce's Jerry Lewis inspired telephone technician act.

JB: What are your thoughts on Lee's acting, in general?

AC: His acting skills have always been eclipsed by his cult of personality. There is a tendency to view Bruce's screen characters as interchangeable or part of one big continuum because of their shared physical characteristics (i.e., hairstyle, facial gestures, combat stances, war cries.) This has resulted in him never being truly recognized as an actor, but a martial athlete who brought his existing persona to each film. In truth, he was a legitimately versatile performer, who's commitment to character is apparent throughout all his work. Cheng Chao-Ahn in The Big Boss is radically different from Chen Zhen in Fist of Fury. Way of the Dragon's Tang Lung is, in part, an ode to Charlie Chaplin. Lee infuses Lee Jun Keung, in Enter the Dragon, with a Steve McQueen swagger that redefines the term 'King of Cool.' And with The Orphan, Bruce absolutely slays the rebellious, 'bad boy with a heart of gold' archetype with a performance worthy of James Dean.

JB: Speaking of The Orphan, I know you brought the film for a limited screening to the US in 2018. How'd you come to be involved with that?

AC: I first became aware of The Orphan in 1980, after seeing a collection of movie stills in the book Bruce Lee, The Untold Story. The photos caught my attention because they presented Bruce as a sneering young rebel who carried a switchblade and actively sought out confrontations (I'm smiling as I type this, because it's a reminder of how often life imitates art.) Though tagged as one of his childhood movies, it's not, given that it was made when he was eighteen years old and legally an adult. Over the years I learned that the film's copy right holders had no interest in releasing it through conventional media outlets. In 2018, I was able to connect with them through a mutual contact in Hong Kong, and, upon hearing my ideas, they agreed to lend me The Orphan for two screenings that I did in New York and Seattle. It was a wonderful opportunity to reintroduce the picture to US audiences since it first played here the early 1960's, and, for me, both thrilling and eye-opening to see Bruce's amazing performance – which gives viewers a much better understanding of the depths of his acting talent.

JB: Another thing you brought back from Game of Death '78 was John Barry's score. Was there another soundtrack (from any other artist or any other Bruce Lee film) that you could have sourced? Runners up? Can you elaborate on the teaser's piano theme as well?

AC: Game of Death is a highly expressionistic piece. Its action possesses a musical, almost lyrical, cadence that relates to Hai Tien's physical and emotional journey within the story. John Barry's soundtrack is a master class in how music honors and affects the emotional core of a film. My impetus in creating Redux was contingent on using his score, so no, I never considered another composer's work. With the teaser trailer, I wanted to musically reflect the story's central theme. I fell in love with the piano rendition of Barry's music, which was not only incredibly atmospheric, but complementary to the surreal elements in Lee's imagery. Stylistically speaking, the teaser does a decent job of distinguishing Redux from its predecessors. I recall you messaging me upon first seeing it. What were your thoughts and how did it affect you?

JB: Being a huge fan of John Barry's composition for Game of Death, the Teaser trailer for Redux, especially its low/slow tempo, piano-driven take, sent goosebumps up my spine. It's another example that – even in Trailers – music is one of the legs that holds any moving picture up. The Art Port "guitar" rendition of John Barry's score, and the lack of John Barry's composition in Warriors Journey, are those projects' biggest flaws. With that said, where exactly did you hitch the piano score for the Teaser?

AC: It's the work of a musician named Hajp, who's YouTube channel I was fortunate enough to come across a few years ago. Hajp was very forthcoming and happy to be part of the project. He has covered themes from all of Bruce's adult films, as well as many other popular tunes. If you're into piano music, I recommend checking his page out.

JB: Earlier, you mentioned a musical cadence to Game of Death. Can you elaborate on that?

AC: Bruce was a dancer, so music was hugely influential on his artistic expression and approach to screen combat. His cinematic battles often had a poetic pulse that guided the subtext within the narrative. I'm certain this aspect of his choreography would've continued to develop with each project.
https://www.youtube.com/watch?v=ZSXPzjtKBPs

JB: Do you think, if Bruce had completed Game in 1972/1973, that he would have had Joseph Koo to score the film, like some fans seem to believe? It's not a stretch, given he loved what Koo did in Way of the Dragon.

AC: No doubt, Bruce loved Koo's score and, as you're aware, played percussion on the main theme for Way of the Dragon. Predictably, this has led some shortsighted fans to surmise that Koo's work would have served as the musical template for all of Lee's movies. This way of thinking governed John Little's choice of music in Warriors Journey. The inherent problem with that model is that it fails to acknowledge that Bruce was an evolving artist – in the most complete sense of the term – and certainly wouldn't have limited his palette to one specific style of music. Given that Game of Death was intended for the international market, it's difficult to see him going with Koo, especially having just come off Lalo Schifrin's operatic score for Enter the Dragon. Koo's music, while memorable, was more understated.

JB: Do you think Lee might have eventually used popular music in his movies?

AC: Great question. Stewart Copeland, one of the world's preeminent drummers, and founder of the rock group The Police, took his artistry to the next level when he began composing for film. His approach to percussion was both unorthodox and personal. I think Lee would have been a big admirer of The Police and seen a lot of himself in Copeland. So, the long answer is, yeah, he probably would have.

JB: If Lee had finished filming the entire pagoda sequence, how do you think those battles would compare to the three we know and love?

AC: My feeling is the 'Hall of the Praying Mantis' would have had the potential to be the crown jewel in Lee's fight choreography. Following the motif of Hai Tien beating each guardian at their own game, this duel would have served as a postmodern critique of his mother art, Wing Chun, with Bruce highlighting many of the modifications he made to the system in the early 1960's. From a visual perspective, the praying mantis shapes would also have provided a nice artistic touch to the close quarter combat. I should also stress that had Bruce completed Game of Death, the filmed sequence would have been whittled down to an even shorter running time than Redux. With an additional sixteen to twenty minutes of action coming from the two preceding battles, the pacing of the pagoda finale would have been an entirely different animal. Having said that, the short film structure of Redux works well with the footage coming in at a 31:46 run time.

JB: For years, there has been ongoing speculation on what the treasure at the top of the pagoda would have been. Given your attention to theme and symbolism, would you care to throw your hat in the ring on this?

AC: The treasure is the ultimate McGuffin. Many believe that Lee would have taken the 'mirror book' idea from the The Silent Flute and applied it to the ending of Game of Death. I don't think it would have worked. Why? Because that kind of outcome only holds weight if the protagonist's intent is to acquire the object directly for his or herself. Contrary to this, Hai Tien's goal is to clear the path that leads to the treasure, and not the treasure itself. His sole concern is the safety of his family. In my script treatment, I give a few thoughts on what the treasure could be, but, fundamentally, I believe it's far more effective for the audience not to know [similar to the way Tarantino used the briefcase in Pulp Fiction.]

> "I don't consider myself a "Bruce Lee Historian." The caption has all the makings of an SNL joke. I mean, when it comes to another individual's life, who can truly lay claim to that title? You either know some shit, or you don't. But no matter how much you know; you can't know everything. If the Bob Baker letters taught us anything, it's that."

JB: Speaking of Quentin Tarantino, what do you think of his controversial portrayal of Bruce Lee in Once Upon a Time in Hollywood?

AC: I'm a huge fan of Tarantino's work. I have no issue with the fictitious Cliff Booth besting Bruce in a fight. Even if he weren't a fictional character, it is possible that he, or someone like him, could have beaten Lee. That's how it goes in the real world. Where Quentin drops the ball is in his depiction of Bruce's character as a loudmouth jerk who actively picks a fight with a stuntman on a professional film set.

JB: As with many other "Bruce Lee Historians" – you have a strong opinion on Bruce Lee and his work, particularly Game of Death '72, with your upcoming Game of Death Redux. With that said, how would you reply to being another "white men in Hollywood trying to tell me who Bruce Lee was"?

AC: I don't consider myself a "Bruce Lee Historian." The caption has all the makings of an SNL joke. I mean, when it comes to another individual's life, who can truly lay claim to that title? You either know some shit, or you don't. But no matter how much you know, you'll never know everything. If the Bob Baker letters taught us anything, it's that. To answer your question, I find it ironic that white men are targeted, given the fact that the individual who said it is three-fourths Caucasian herself (not to mention that her father was Eurasian.) Moreover, it's insulting to the numerous Caucasians, who were friends, students, and business associates of Bruce Lee. One of them, Jay Sebring, was solely responsible for connecting Bruce to Hollywood. Another, Stirling Silliphant, wrote vehicles to showcase Bruce's talent in TV and Film. If I'm perceived to be part of that tribe, then I would say I'm in good company.

JB: Makes sense. With that said, do you consider yourself a Game of Death historian?

AC: If I am, it's by default, not by design.

JB: Have you communicated with anyone who was involved with the previous Game of Death edits?

AC: No, but I was bemused that Bey Logan, of all people, commented on Redux's trailer, saying something to the effect of, in today's world, an Asian actor should have voiced Bruce's dialogue. Given Bey's history, I find his attempt to be politically correct unbefitting, not to mention contributory to the stereotype that Asians categorically speak a specific way.

JB: How about John Little?

AC: I've had no communication with John. I think some people assume that I dislike him when nothing could be further from the truth. I respect his efforts with Warriors Journey.

JB: Are there any specific Bruce Lee project (books, documentaries, commentaries) that you have appreciated lately? If so, can you mention them?

AC: In recent years, there are a few worth mentioning. Matthew Polly's Bruce Lee: A Life is the best biography on Lee ever written – I'm talking head and shoulders above the rest. I enjoyed Darren Chua and Steve Kerridge's Mandarin Superstar and Intercepting Fist books which document the making of The Big Boss and Fist of Fury. The Silent Flutebook by Marcos

Ocana is an excellent window into the creative process of three talented men and their efforts to get the project to the big screen, as well as a candid chronicle of the dissolution of the friendship between Lee and Coburn. As far as documentaries, my favorites remain 1984's The Legend and 1991's Curse of the Dragon, though I also dig 1973's The Man and the Legend and 1994's A&E Biography. There aren't many commentaries that hold my attention all the way through, but I did enjoy Brandon Bentley's take on The Big Boss. It's the best one out there, thus far.

JB: With regards to James Coburn and Bruce's friendship – what happened there?

AC: The relationship was complex. The Silent Flute came about during a period when Bruce was on the fringe of achieving his Hollywood dream. He relied on Coburn and Silliphant's influence in Tinseltown to anchor the project and provide him with a shot at movie stardom. Had it materialized, one of Bruce's many contributions to the production would've been his singular vision for the film's fight choreography.

Actors, though, are highly competitive by nature, and the sex appeal that Lee exuded when performing combat for the camera would pose a threat to any male co-star - including James Coburn. Not wanting to be outshined by Bruce, Coburn took the precautionary measure of signing on to direct the film to ensure he retained some level of control over the final product.

JB: That's interesting, I never knew that Coburn was initially going to direct the project.

AC: As the story evolved, Coburn abandoned his directorial aspirations, astutely discerning that the picture needed a seasoned filmmaker to successfully translate the material to the big screen. But the dynamic between Lee and Coburn created its own mini-drama and set the stage for a bad break up between the two men, culminating with Bruce blaming Jim for blowing the deal and expressing regret over partnering with him in the first place. When assessing these events, this also matters: Coburn and Silliphant initially approached Bruce to learn the way of combat - an arena in which they perceived him to be the absolute authority, both physically and philosophically. However, in their pursuit to finance the film, the dynamic of that relationship shifted. In the world of cinema, James Coburn was the Hollywood star, Stirling Silliphant, the award-winning screenwriter and Bruce Lee, the unproven commodity. The deviation in hierarchy was not lost on Bruce, and he was extremely uncomfortable in a situation where he was perceived to be the low man on the totem pole. During their trip to India, Lee lived in the shadow of Coburn's celebrity among the star struck locals, and often felt powerless in the decision-making process. The experience left him disappointed in Silliphant, resentful of Coburn and less connected to the script. It was a bitterness he would never fully shake, even after his monumental success in Hong Kong. In retrospect, it's clear that Hollywood's social scale played a significant role in disrupting their relationship.

JB: Didn't Coburn visit him in HK to try and get The Silent Flute running again?

AC: When Coburn visited Hong Kong, Lee was more interested in showing off his success to his former student than he was in discussing any future collaboration on The Silent Flute. He reveled in the fact that the tables had turned, and that he was now the one being pursued by Coburn.

JB: Did the recent so-called "Drug Letters" change your opinion on Bruce Lee? Would you consider these controversial?

AC: They haven't changed my opinion in the least. I think much of the shock felt by fans stems from the realization that they can't know everything there is to know about someone they would love to know all there is to know about. Do I consider the letters controversial? Not especially, no.

JB: Acid. Coke. Mushrooms. Etc. Hundreds of dollars' worth (thousands of dollars, given today's inflation). Even Linda Lee was an "accessory". And you're saying this is not controversial?

AC: I don't think the word 'controversial' really applies here. I mean, were drugs controversial with Jimi Hendrix and Elvis Presley? **Make no mistake, in the last year of his life, Bruce was a bona-fide Rock Star. And he lived the life of a Rock Star. In that respect, he had more in common with Jim Morrison than Lao Tzu.** To understand these missives, one must examine the rise of drug culture between 1968-1973, and how it shaped Western society. In the early 1970s, scientifically, we knew much less about the consequences of cocaine than in the "just say no" era that followed. Back then, Hollywood, not only embraced cocaine (despite its illegal status) but actively promoted it as fashionable and desirable. Hard to believe, but true.

JB: And what would you say to those who turned their back on Bruce after reading those letters?

AC: That type of reaction comes from an unhealthy projection and worship of Lee's screen image. At the end of the day, it's a misplaced sense of betrayal that's unfair to everyone involved. Like many before and after him, Bruce was a young man in the process of discovering who he was. He was also quite impressionable - by fashion, music, and cinema. Showbiz exposed him to a few vices. It's not shocking when viewed through that lens.

"Make no mistake, in the last year of his life, Bruce was a bona-fide Rock Star. And he lived the life of a Rock Star. In that respect, he had more in common with Jim Morrison than Lao Tzu"

JB: If Bruce Lee would have lived after the release of Enter the Dragon, what do you think his next few years would look like in the Hollywood/Hong Kong movie industry?

AC: I don't think he would have continued to film Game of Death with Golden Harvest. The 1972 footage would probably have never seen the light of day, though it would've certainly been used as a blueprint for the big budget version he would've made in Hollywood. Based on the success of Enter the Dragon, it's likely he would have made another film with Robert Clouse. The Shaw Bros. Wuxia project which spawned the famous photoshoot of Lee in various period costumes would have been kicked down the road, if made at all, as its highly doubtful that he would have remained in Hong Kong following the mega success of Enter the Dragon. He may have entertained doing a picture with the Shaw's after his first box office failure though. Beyond that, I think career-wise he would have been typecast for a while, much like Stallone and Eastwood. And like them, he would have continued to reinvent himself.

JB: So, sequels for Dirty Harry, French Connection, The Godfather and Shaft were made around this time. Do you think Clouse and Lee would have teamed up for a straight sequel to Enter?

AC: It would be difficult to do a worthy sequel to Enter. In many ways, it was the perfect cinematic introduction of Lee to the West and didn't lend itself to another viable adventure. Would you have liked to see one?

JB: Who wouldn't like to have seen an Enter the Dragon 2? Han would have some heirs that would set up a nice revenge-driven plot. Despite the complaint that John Saxon gets far too much screen time in Enter is something that could have been fixed in its sequel. Besides, Bruce and John did share some good onscreen chemistry. The bond they develop is made evident in the film's tail end before the credits roll.

AC: Bruce and John did have great screen chemistry! I will admit to being intrigued by the less addressed dynamic between Lee and Williams. Although the characters never converse with each other, there's a distinct peripheral awareness, a vibe, that comes across between the two men.

JB: What are some of the biggest misconceptions about Bruce Lee that you think the world needs to know?

AC: Bruce Lee is perceived by most of his fans as a philosopher and a fighter. He was neither. A more accurate description of him would be an incredible performer who studied some philosophy and became an excellent martial artist.

JB: What about the perception of him as a teacher?

AC: Bruce never really enjoyed teaching. What he liked was the reverence it awarded him. That's what made the experience tolerable. Later, when he became Sifu to the stars, the aim was to impress his A-list Hollywood clientele in hopes of breaking into movies and becoming a star.

JB: How do you feel about the direction the Bruce Lee Estate has taken with Bruce's legacy?

AC: They've gone to great lengths to create an image of him that's firmly rooted in the characters he played in Longstreet and Enter the Dragon. Unfortunately, this narrative eschews the wonderfully complex human being Bruce Lee was in real life.

The recent documentary Be Water, is a good example of this, only it adds insult to injury by attempting to define Bruce's entire adult life as a struggle against racism.

In doing so, it turns Lee into a caricature and reduces his story to fit the filmmaker's agenda.

JB: So, I take it you don't own any hoodies or coffee mugs that read "Be like water, my friend"?

AC: Alas, no. I do, however, own an awesome Daffy Duck baseball cap! How 'bout you?

"The recent documentary Be Water, is a good example of this, only it adds insult to injury by attempting to define Bruce's entire adult life as a struggle against racism"

JB: My DVD copy of Bruce Li's Bruce Lee the Man/The Myth says more than a "Be Like Water" hoodie. If you were given total control of the Bruce Lee Estate, what new directions would you steer it in?

AC: Personally, I would focus more on his cinematic legacy. His process as an actor, choreographer and filmmaker has yet to be fully examined. Even his childhood films. This is crucial to understanding Bruce as a person and as an artist. To me, he remains a 20th Century Dorian Gray figure.

JB: We've seen the Teaser for Game of Death Redux. We've seen the Trailer for Game of Death Redux. Now, when we will see the Game of Death Redux in its full glory?

AC: I'm thrilled to report that I'm currently working with a prominent UK label that is well known for the standard of excellence it brings to each of its projects. I can't reveal any details yet, but it promises to be spectacular. I'm sure the usual suspects will be very happy. Tangentially, I'm also in discussions with some of the major streaming platforms. Release dates are still TBD but keep your eye out for some awesome stuff this year.

Thanks again to Alan Canvan for taking the time to have this discussion. Be on the lookout for his upcoming Game of Death Redux, which will be announced soon.

The Game of Death

死亡的遊戲

www.ingramcontent.com/pod-product-compliance
Lightning Source LLC
Chambersburg PA
CBHW042020090526
44590CB00029B/4343